W9-ASC-470

THE
GOURMET
GARDEN

THE GOURMET GARDEN

Virginia Hayes

GLEN ELLYN PUBLIC LIBRARY
400 DUANE STREET
GLEN ELLYN, ILLINOIS 60137

A QUINTET BOOK

First edition for the United States and Canada
published in 2008 by Barron's Educational Series, Inc.

Copyright © 2008 Quintet Publishing Limited

All rights reserved. No part of this publication may be
reproduced or distributed in any form or by any means
without the written permission of the copyright owner.

All inquiries should be addressed to:
Barron's Educational Series, Inc.
250 Wireless Boulevard
Hauppauge, NY 11788
www.barronseduc.com

Library of Congress Control Number: 2008929990

ISBN-13: 978-0-7641-4001-3

QTT.GOG

Conceived, designed, and produced by
Quintet Publishing Limited
The Old Brewery
6 Blundell Street
London N7 9BH
UK

Project editors: Marianne Canty, Asha Savjani
Designer: Bonnie Bryan
Copy editor: Richard Rosenfeld
Illustrator: Bernard Chau
Editorial assistant: Robert Davies
Art director: Sofia Henry
Managing editor: Donna Gregory
Publisher: James Tavendale

Manufactured by Pica Digital, Singapore
Printed by SNP Leefung, China

9 8 7 6 5 4 3 2 1

Contents

Introduction

Connoisseurs of good food know that it isn't just about how you prepare a dish, but also the quality of ingredients used. Although produce displayed in markets is perfectly safe to eat, many products these days have lost much of their former flavor and texture. Commercial agriculture has substituted stewardship of healthy and diverse ecosystems with the use of chemical fertilizers and disease suppression methods that essentially sterilize the soil and kill both pests and beneficial organisms alike. Modern horticulturists have also bred (by time-honored methods as well as by genetic modification technology) crops that thrive in this environment, but that may have lost much of their taste and even their highest potential nutritional value. In some cases the old species and varieties may have been lost, but increasingly, grassroots movements to preserve them have gained momentum, and now they are being grown and perpetuated for a wider audience. Their unique germplasm is preserved for future needs, and gardeners are able to choose from a wide variety of vegetables, herbs, and fruit that suit their particular tastes and growing conditions. In a world increasingly turning to mass-produced and gene-altered food products, gourmet cooks are turning to their own gardens for more healthy alternatives— organically grown and freshly harvested.

Not only will the methods employed in organic gardening produce healthier food, but they are better for the overall health of the neighborhood and the planet, too. Incorporating living compost into the soil increases the biodiversity of soil microorganisms. Many of them form intimate relationships with roots to increase their ability to utilize water and nutrients. Mulching with organic materials adds additional organic matter to fuel the nutrient cycle in which the essential elements contained in dead plant material are made available to the next generation of plants. This healthy soil produces healthier plants that can resist pathogens and pests. Ceasing to kill both beneficial insects as well as the occasional aphid or cabbage moth with chemical controls and tolerating small outbreaks of pests will also lead to a more natural ecosystem with its own checks and balances. By employing these sustainable methods, even home gardeners can contribute to a positive change toward a healthier community.

Another advantage to growing your own produce is the reduction in time and energy expended in getting food from the field to the kitchen. Mega-farms must ship their products many miles to processing centers and then even more miles to distribution hubs and finally to the local store. Individual shoppers must leave their homes and travel to those shops and back again to secure their family's dinner. The more food that can be grown at home, the far fewer miles that cars, trucks, and trains, even airplanes, must cover to deliver it, resulting in a large reduction in the carbon footprint required to eat well.

The instant that a tomato is picked, a carrot unearthed or a sprig of rosemary plucked, the vibrant forces of life begin to ebb. A multi-armed industry has risen around the need to preserve food for future consumption. Refrigeration, pickling, canning, freezing, and fermentation are all used in many applications to ensure the healthful consumption of food. Homegrown produce is the freshest available, coming directly from the garden to the kitchen with maximum vitamins, color, and flavor. By growing food at home and in community gardens, these qualities can be retained and enjoyed without that additional expenditure of energy.

In addition, there is often no substitute for a particular ingredient to achieve the desired flavor. Fresh fruits and vegetables play an important role in many epicurean delights. For many cooks, the specialty foods shops are even farther away than their usual food markets. The stores themselves may be literally half a world away from the farms that produced the essential flavors for a dish. This is, of course, true for cooks trying to replicate recipes from around the world, but can also apply to cooks in rural or suburban areas. These indispensable ingredients are prime candidates for the home garden.

Novice, as well as experienced, gardeners and cooks will find information on growing their own healthful and flavorful gourmet ingredients here. There are chapters on cultivating and using greens and leafy vegetables, herbs, edible flowers, heirloom vegetables and their baby versions, along with special ingredients for your favorite ethnic dishes—even how to grow your own mushrooms. The basic techniques of organic gardening methods as well as other instructions on building raised beds, utilizing cold frames and row covers to extend the season, pruning for greater production and overall plant health, as well as finding the right place for each plant and providing them with a companion to enhance production and health, are detailed. Readers will also find tips on including all of this tasty produce in gourmet dishes.

Virginia Hayes

Techniques

There are various methods for growing different varieties of plants as well as preserving, storing, and using them.

Container gardening

For any plant to thrive, it must receive the right amount of light, water, and nutrients. It also needs to be grown in a zone where temperatures are neither too hot nor too cold for its particular requirements, and the soil type must correspond to that in which the particular species evolved. All of these conditions can be met when using containers.

Container growing

Even if you haven't got space for lots of beds, many gourmet ingredients are easily grown in containers that can be positioned near the kitchen. Container growing also means that you can provide each plant with its own special needs. So, herbs native to dry, well-drained soils in the Mediterranean (including sage, thyme, and lavender) can be given a light, open soil, and those requiring heavier ground can be given soil with much more body. Group together plants requiring similar conditions and provide the right microclimate.

Planting a container

1 Choose a container, such as a drum, gallon can, tub, or wooden box. The size will vary according to the space available and the plant you are growing.

2 Add about 1 inch (2.5 cm) of coarse gravel to the bottom of the container to provide drainage for the growing plants.

3 Fill the container with lightweight peat compost.

4 Transplant young plants when they have 2 or 3 leaves. Make a hole in the compost with your finger. Place the plant in carefully. Secure in place by firming the compost around the stem.

5 Water the container with water mixed with a little liquid fertilizer. Keep the plants watered every day. Take care not to allow the compost to dry out.

SEEDLINGS

Once a seedling starts to photosynthesize, it is no longer dependent on the seed's energy reserves. The apical meristems start growing and give rise to the root and shoot. Leaves begin to develop.

Germinating seeds

If you want to grow your vegetables and herbs from seed, you need to allow them to germinate before planting them in containers.

1 Sow the seed in a plastic tray, pot, or cardboard egg carton filled with compost, or use peat pellets or peat pots, which you can buy from local nursery supply centers.

2 Cover the seeds with ¼–½ inch (5 mm–1 cm) of compost. Cover the container with plastic film and leave in a warm sunny place for 4–8 weeks. By then, the first few leaves should be appearing and the plants will be ready to be transplanted into containers outdoors.

Designing a vegetable garden

Vegetable garden design is important if you want to get the most from your planting. You need to think about the size of your garden, the amount of sunlight it receives, and the vegetables you want to plant. Before planting a single seed, you need to put your ideas down on paper to check their viability.

Size of your garden

The amount of space you give over to your vegetable plot will depend on your interest in gardening, the amount of time you can give to looking after it, and the actual space available. Some gardeners like to use all the available space for vegetables, whereas others use only a small corner. If you are gardening on a balcony or patio, you won't have any choice to begin with. It is worth remembering that the larger your garden, the more time and work you are going to have to put into it. If you are unused to vegetable gardening, my advice is to start small and let the vegetable garden size increase as your confidence and interest develops.

Choosing vegetables

First you need to make a list of the vegetables you want to plant. Check when you need to plant them. When are their harvest dates? It is best to choose a range of vegetables with different harvesting dates so your plot will always have some plants in and your vegetables will not all be ready at the same time. You will need to map out successive plantings. Will they all fit? Some vegetables, such as cucumbers, take up a lot of space, and you might need to rethink your ideas. Perhaps you can exploit vertically climbing plants —using trellis and canes—in addition to sprawling ones, if you do not have much space.

Choosing a site

You need to use your common sense here. Not all parts of your garden may be ideal for growing vegetables. Try to avoid steep slopes, areas prone to flooding, and those too far away from a water supply. The best site is in full sun, and sheltered from wind. Ensure the area is weed-free and at least 10–20 yards (10–20 m) from large tree roots. Make sure you put down a thick layer of mulch to conserve water and kill weeds before planting. Before deciding on the exact dimensions of your plot, you need to consider which vegetables you would like to plant.

Drawing up a plan

It might sound like a lot of work to draw up a plan, but it is worth it in the long run. Use a sheet of squared paper so that you can work to scale.

1 Measure your garden space and plot it on graph paper, using a scale that suits you. A commonly used scale is 1 inch (2.5 cm) of paper to 8 feet (2.4 m) of garden space, but you can adapt the scale to whatever is easiest for you. Remember, there isn't a law that requires your garden to be square or rectangular. Your garden can be round, curved, or any other shape that fits your landscape or inclination.

2 Plot the areas for planting and areas for paths. In a small garden, plant in wide rows or in solid blocks 4–5 feet (1.2–1.5 m) wide. You must be able to reach the center of each row from either side. Bear in mind that if you decide on long, straight rows, you'll need to lay down wooden planks when you access your plants, so as not to step on them. If planting on either side of a central path, it must be wide enough to push a wheelbarrow along without disturbing your plants.

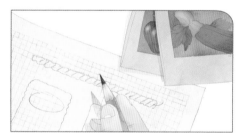

3 Start the plan by sketching in cool-season varieties of vegetables you want to plant. Sketch circles to represent individual transplants, and rows for directly sown seeds. Take care in placing the vegetables. Place taller plants in the north or northeast area of the garden so they won't shade other plants as they grow.

4 Calculate when these cool-season varieties will mature so that you can replace them with warm-season crops. Draw another plan to indicate the second planting.

Keeping records

Keeping good records is a part of ongoing planning, and you should build your records the same way you build your garden; profit from past mistakes and incorporate new ideas. Keep a daily record, noting such things as soil preparation, planting, weeding, fertilizing, flowering dates, ripening dates, and the results. Note problems with weeds, pests, or rainfall, and if the harvest of each item was sufficient. At the end of the growing season, you'll have a complete record of what you did, and this information will give you the basis for planning next year's garden.

Companion plants

There are some plants that seem to perform better when in the presence of other species. Gardeners have been exploiting this fact for a long time, and old texts and gardening lore refer to "companion plants"—two or more types that will thrive when grown in each other's company. Not only do the plants seem to grow better, but they are often insect-free whereas if planted alone they might be plagued with pests. Leeks and celery are one such happy pair, as are green beans and Swiss chard, lettuce and kohlrabi, and carrots and tomatoes.

Conversely, there are a few plants that don't mix well together. Some are just thirstier than others and need to be kept to themselves, and some hungry plants (including broccoli, cucumber, cabbage, pumpkins, eggplant, watermelon, and squash) don't want any competition or they end up putting on weak growth. Others, such as walnut trees, may even produce root exudates that are poisonous to their neighbors. Whatever the reason, don't plant onions near asparagus, and peas (or green beans or kohlrabi) next to tomatoes. Potatoes and pumpkins need to be separated, and dill should never be grown next to carrots. Other bad combinations include sage and cucumbers, cabbage and strawberries, and beets and green beans.

Crop rotation

At its most basic level, crop rotation is not difficult to achieve and can make gardening more interesting, as it will change the appearance of your garden each season. However, it has many important functions, and is also essential for the health of your soil.

Reasons to rotate

There are three main purposes behind the concept of crop rotation:

- To prevent attacks from insects, pests, and other diseases.
- To deter weed growth. Some crops, such as potatoes and squashes, can suppress weeds, thereby minimizing problems for crops following on.
- To maintain soil fertility. Changing crops from year to year minimizes deficiencies and allows the soil to replenish.
- To improve soil structure, which is achieved by alternating shallow-rooted crops with deep-rooted ones.

If you grow the same plants in the same spot in the garden, year after year, you will be making the same yearly demands on the soil, allowing fungi, viruses, and bacteria to thrive during the growing season. In order to counter pests and diseases, it is important to establish a crop rotation pattern. This simply means moving groups of plants around in sequence, so they don't return to the same spot for at least three years.

Crop rotation might seem too complicated or impractical for the average garden, but it does not have to be. It can be achieved by following one basic rule: Don't plant the same crop in the same place two years running.

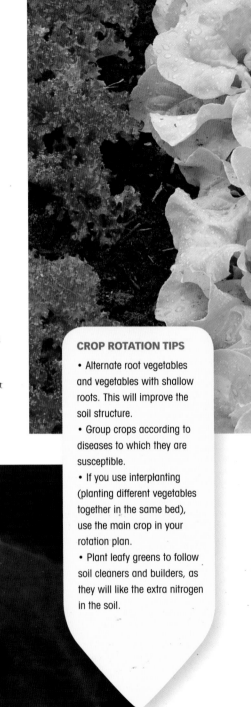

CROP ROTATION TIPS

- Alternate root vegetables and vegetables with shallow roots. This will improve the soil structure.
- Group crops according to diseases to which they are susceptible.
- If you use interplanting (planting different vegetables together in the same bed), use the main crop in your rotation plan.
- Plant leafy greens to follow soil cleaners and builders, as they will like the extra nitrogen in the soil.

Plant groups

As certain plants are related to each other, it is important to understand how the groups differ, so that you don't plant members of the same family in successive seasons in the same spot. Each group of plants needs completely different nutrients from the soil, so to keep the soil healthy you need to rotate the location of each group every year. There are four distinct groups of plants:

- Leafy vegetables
- Fruits
- Root vegetables
- Soil cleaners and builders

Leafy vegetables

This group includes lettuce, cauliflower, cabbage, spinach, broccoli, and salad greens. They thrive on nitrogen from the soil.

Fruits

These include tomatoes, peppers, cucumbers, and melons. They thrive on phosphorus from the soil.

Root vegetables

Examples include carrots, onions, leeks, radishes, rutabaga, and parsnips. These thrive on potassium.

Soil cleaners and builders

Examples include potatoes, corn, peas, and beans. This plant group stores the nitrogen from the air and then it is released into the soil.

To rotate these crops, follow a pattern of planting leafy vegetables the first season. Follow successive seasons with fruits, root plants, and finally your soil builders and cleaners. This will ensure you are establishing a good crop rotation system.

By following this system, the yield from the crops you plant will be greater and of better quality, and your soil will be much healthier.

How to rotate crops

1 Divide your garden into sections or beds that are roughly the same size. If you plan to use a 4-year rotation, divide the garden into beds that are a multiple of 4. For a 3-year rotation, use multiples of 3.

2 Group plants of the same family in the same bed. If you don't have enough of one crop to fill a section, combine crop groups with compatible needs. For example, plant leafy greens and shallow-rooted vegetables to fill in spaces.

3 When the crop is harvested, replant the section or bed with a crop from another plant group. Remember to keep a record from year to year of your crop rotations.

Gardening inside

If you have no room outside for growing plants, you can still grow some vegetables and herbs indoors. You can also successfully transfer herbs indoors for the winter. Apart from rosemary, most culinary herbs adapt well to the indoor environment during the winter months, provided they receive the right conditions. Turn the pots every few days to avoid the plants developing a lopsided look.

INDOOR TEMPERATURE CONTROL

It's harder than you might think to keep control of indoor temperatures—central heating, sunny windowsills, and drafts can all lead to hot and cold spots in your home. Plants like constant temperatures, so try to find spaces inside where the temperature won't vary too much. Also, remember to water daily if necessary.

Transferring herbs indoors

You can use this technique for chives and parsley.

1 Divide a portion of the growing herbs with a sharp trowel. Pull the clump out of the ground, taking care to get as many roots as possible.

2 Plant the herb clump in a container filled with potting mix and firm the mixture around the roots with your fingers. Water the herbs well.

3 Trim away up to two-thirds of the top growth with scissors. This will make them grow much faster. Place the herbs in a south- or west-facing window.

Taking cuttings

Use this technique for perennial herbs such as marjoram, mint, oregano, and thyme.

1 At the end of the growing season, cut a 6-in. (15-cm) section of herb stem, and remove the lower leaves. Ideally you should have 6 or 8 sets of leaves above the cut.

2 Place the cutting in a container filled with perlite, coarse sand, or a combination of the two. You don't need to dip herb cuttings in a rooting hormone because all herbs will root without it.

3 Water the plant well and cover with a plastic bag. Place the container in a cool, dimly lit area indoors. Virtually all herbs will take root between 3 and 6 weeks. At this point, remove the bag.

Indoor gardening essentials

- Do not use soil from the garden for your indoor plants. Use potting mix.
- Rotate your plants to promote straight growth.
- Pay attention to lighting requirements. If plants appear thin and leggy, they need extra light.
- Water your plants with water at room temperature. Soak thoroughly but don't allow them to sit in water, as this will cause root rot.
- Bathe your plants occasionally to get rid of dust and dirt. Place in the kitchen sink and rinse leaves with lukewarm water, using a spray attachment.
- Allow fresh air into the house several times a week, as plants suffer in stale air.
- Don't overheat your house. Most plants thrive in a daytime temperature of 65–75°F (18–23°C).
- Label each of your plants so you remember what it is and what type of care it needs.
- Feed your indoor plants often during the growing season because vital nutrients are flushed out of the soil each time you water.
- When you notice the plant roots coming through the drainage holes, repot into a bigger container.

Creating an indoor salad garden

It is also possible to grow certain vegetables indoors. Some easy greens to grow are lettuce, snap peas, chives, spinach, mustard greens, and radishes.

1 Fill a seedling tray with soil-less potting mix or seeding mix, then water.

2 Sow seeds in the tray at the correct depth. See the seed packet for instructions, as the depth will vary depending on which seeds you are planting. Water the soil and label the seeds.

3 Place the tray in a south- or west-facing window provided it is warm enough and there isn't a cold air draft. Seeds need to be warm enough to germinate.

4 Once the seeds have germinated, replant them into 4-in. (10-cm) pots to give them room to grow. Keep a light on young plants to prevent leggy growth; they need 12 to 14 hours of light each day.

5 Harvest your fresh greens by pinching off the leaves as you need them, which will promote new growth. Replant as you harvest, to ensure a continuous supply of salad.

Pathways

When designing any garden project, make sure that there is good access so that you can dig out weeds, haul a load of mulch or compost to the planting bed, or harvest a crop, without stepping on and ruining the structure of the soil. Wood chips, gravel, bricks, terra-cotta tiles, and flagstones are all suitable materials for making a path.

All paths should be smooth and level, and be designed to drain off irrigation and rainwater quickly for safe and secure footing in all weather. Ideally, paths should be maintenance-free, allowing more time for you to devote to your fruit and vegetable crops.

Stepping-stones

A simpler solution than making a path, stepping-stones provide an effective way to access a large flower bed. Place several large, flat stones in the soil where required. Ensure the gaps between the stones are not so wide that they cause difficulty when walking over the stones.

Making a path

1 Work out the width of the path—ideally wide enough to take a wheelbarrow. You can mark the edges with pegs and string if you want straight lines. Otherwise use stones, bricks, or other edging, to define the area.

2 Using a rake, level out the path area, ensuring that rainwater can drain away easily for safe and secure footing in all weather.

3 For a pretty cottage-garden look, cover the surface of the path evenly with wood chips or other organic mulch or gravel.

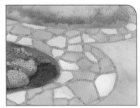

4 Alternatively, lay bricks, flagstones, or terra-cotta tiles in a neat or random pattern over the surface. Fill in any gaps with thyme and gravel.

EDGING

Edging helps to contain the soil and provides a visual separation between the path and the bed. Bricks laid on edge to create a dog-tooth pattern is a popular and attractive form of edging.

STAKING CLIMBERS
Many plants, such as climbing French beans, have no means of support and are best kept in line by actually tying them to a trellis or another fence-like structure. There are various other utilitarian or ornamental options in wood, plastic, and metal to choose from.

Staking and tying

Sometimes it's necessary to stake newly planted trees and shrubs to prevent them from being blown over, or damaged by mowers. For fruit- and vegetable-bearing plants, support is particularly important to prevent their falling over and their crops being damaged.

Many plants need some support to hold up their flowers and fruit. If the plant is rather shrubby and multi-stemmed, like tomatoes, consider a simple cylinder of fencing material (either plastic or metal) to enclose the clump and provide resting places for individual stems. It's best to put these in place before the plant reaches its ultimate size so that the plant can grow out through the mesh and hide it.

Single stems, like those of a gladiolus, can be tied to a stake of bamboo or redwood purchased at the local garden supply store, or take a look around your garden and use natural stakes from your fruit tree prunings or other tree-trimming projects. Not only do these blend into the scene rather better, but they recycle green waste.

Staking a vine

Vines are different, and just need something to lean on. Many vines climb by twining either their growing tip (in the case of cucumbers and beans) or specialized tendrils (peas and grapes) around whatever they can. Those that climb upward by means of tendrils that curl around whatever they touch, are easily held up by plastic netting or fine-gauge metal fencing suspended between fence posts.

For those vines that have twining stems, larger-diameter poles (such as bamboo) can be erected. Crossed pairs of poles stabilized with a cross piece at the top, or teepee shapes of three or more poles tied together near the top, may be stable enough to stand on their own.

Staking a plant

1 Select a sturdy, straight stake that is free from splinters. The stake should be tall enough to accommodate the plant's ultimate height, with an allowance to drive it 18–24 inches (45–60 cm) into the ground for stability. Stand the stake beside the plant to determine if it is the proper size.

2 Using a hammer, drive the stake into the ground outside of the drip line of the plant (the imaginary circle on the ground that corresponds to the leaf canopy). If you place the stake too close to the plant, you will damage the roots. Drive the stake into the soil to a depth of 18–24 inches (45–60 cm).

3 Secure the plant to the stake with plastic plant ribbons, coated metal twist ties, grip-lock electrician's ties, natural twine, or soft cotton string. Attach the tie to the stake with a figure eight and secure with a knot or twist. Loop the tie loosely around the plant, cross it over itself in another figure eight, and attach to the stake.

4 An alternative to a figure eight is to secure the tie completely around the stake before looping the plant stem. This works well to keep the tie from slipping down very smooth stakes.

COLD FRAMES

One aim of the cold frame is to protect certain plants at the end of the season from the onset of colder temperatures. Salad crops and other small, cool-growing vegetables and herbs can also thrive in a cold frame through the cool winter months. Sow the seeds or transplant young seedlings into the soil inside the cold frame. It would be prudent to monitor the temperature on sunny days.

Extending seasons

Many vegetable crops are sensitive to cold weather, and the majority of them grow during the frost-free months of the year only. To maximize crop productivity, methods have been developed for extending the season so that gardeners can make the most of their produce.

There are two main ways to extend the season for growing and harvesting food from the garden. One is to start plants indoors before it is safe to plant them in the garden. It is easy to start just a few pots on a windowsill, but if you need more room, try a simple cold frame that can also be used to grow succulent greens and other vegetables through winter. The second way to extend the season is to insulate sensitive plants from the cold by covering them in protective material.

Cold frames

Cold frames work by warming the soil and protecting the plants from the cold weather, rather like a miniature greenhouse. At their most basic, they are low boxes with a transparent top. A typical construction might consist of wooden sides (plywood is fine) with a discarded window frame to create the top. An alternative way to make a cold frame is to throw down four (or more) bales of straw in a square and find a piece of glass or plastic to cover the top.

One major refinement, when building with wood, is to cut the top edges of the sides of the box on a slant. The exact angle isn't too critical, but in winter, when the sun is low in the sky, an angled glass top will capture more solar energy and light than a flat, horizontal one. Since you will need to prop the top open on warm, sunny days, incorporate hinges or use a prop.

Germinating seeds

Cold frames are ideal for germinating seeds in seed trays or other low containers. Even though they aren't sealed or insulated, the air inside will be a few degrees warmer and a little more humid than outside. Seeds will sprout sooner here and require less vigilance to keep them moist.

Once the seeds have germinated, open the top a little to provide better air circulation. As the days grow warmer, open the top to its full extent. As the plants grow close to the size when they can be transplanted into the garden, keep the cold frame open for increasingly longer periods to acclimatize them to the chillier outside world.

Protective materials

Other materials that can be used to protect sensitive plants from the cold range from plastic films to thin layers of spun polyester. They protect plants by holding in a few degrees of heat, and by moderating the extremes of cold. Depending on the thickness you choose, these coverings can provide protection down to $-25^{\circ}F$ ($-32^{\circ}C$). Lay them over wooden frames or plastic pipes to create miniature greenhouses anywhere they are required.

Getting the most out of your cold frame

- Position the box so that it runs east to west, to allow more sun to reach growing plants.
- Slant the glass top so it is lower on the south side and catches more sun.
- Paint the inside of the cold frame white to help reflect sunlight onto the plants.
- Provide ventilation to keep the frame from getting too hot and to reduce dampness inside. Don't allow the temperature to exceed $105^{\circ}F$ ($40^{\circ}C$).
- Block out any air leaks you find, as these will allow warm air to seep out and reduce the effectiveness of the frame.
- To water the plants, use water that is as warm as the soil, as cold water will lower the temperature and reduce the frame's effectiveness.
- On extra cold nights, place small votive candles inside the frame, away from any overhanging leaves.

IMPORTANT DOS AND DON'TS

Do not put the following in your compost bin:

- Cooked vegetables
- Meat
- Dairy products
- Diseased plants
- Dog or cat litter
- Diapers
- Perennial weeds
- Weeds with seedheads
- Plastic, glass, and metals

Any of the above would create unpleasant smells and could encourage unwanted pests. Plastic, glass, and metals do not decompose and must be recycled separately.

Composting

Compost is good for all sorts of things in the garden. Dig it into beds or new planting holes, and when preparing the soil for seeds or transplants. The organic matter both improves soil structure and adds nutrients and a myriad of beneficial organisms. You can also add compost as a topdressing to container plants.

The breakdown of plant parts is the basis of good soil fertility, and affects the health of the complex web of organisms that inhabit it. In nature, leaves, twigs, flowers, fruits, and even whole trees fall to the ground when their season or life is over. They have captured energy from the sun and used it to convert carbon dioxide and water into cellulose and simpler carbohydrates. They have also taken nutrients, such as nitrogen, phosphorus, and potassium, from the soil with other trace mineral necessities, such as iron and manganese, to complete their life cycle. All these elements can, and will, be returned to the soil through the actions of "lower" organisms, such as worms. They don't use it all for themselves, but take a little and leave a lot behind. As they recycle the organic bits that once were part of a rose, for example, so they make the elements available again to a new generation of plants.

Composting organic waste reduces the demands on landfill sites and provides a source of beneficial organic material. In the process of decomposition, a succession of different bacteria will utilize separate components of the material being composted. One helpful by-product of this process is that the compost pile will heat up to such an extent that it will kill any harmful bacteria and fungi, and most weed seeds. Much of the composting cycle can be controlled by the "recipe," or ingredients, used to start the pile. Assembling the right ingredients and monitoring the pile will produce good compost.

Making a compost heap

1 Site your compost heap or bin on a level, well-drained, sunny spot in the garden, preferably screened from the house. In this position, the heap will be accessible for worms to get in and begin working on breaking down the compost. The heat from the sun will help speed up the composting process. The size of your compost heap will depend on the available space.

2 Build up the heap with "greens" such as tea bags, fruit and vegetable peelings, grass clippings, and plant cuttings. These rot fast and provide nitrogen and moisture. You can also compost "browns," such as cardboard egg cartons, fallen leaves, eggshells, and shredded paper. These take longer to break down, but are useful in providing fiber and carbon, as well as air, in the mix.

3 Check your compost heap regularly. If it gets too dry, add more greens; if it becomes too wet, add more browns. Be sure to create air pockets, too, by adding scrunched-up paper or cardboard, and by mixing the compost regularly.

4 After 6–9 months, the compost at the bottom will be dark brown, almost black in color, and with a spongy texture and earthy smell. Spread it on your vegetable beds to improve the quality of the soil by retaining moisture and suppressing weeds.

How a compost heap works

The waste in a compost heap breaks down into nutritious fertilizer over 6–9 months. Initially, microbes start eating the greens. The energy produced as a result increases the temperature of the heap and generates more microbes, and mold starts to appear. Mini-beasts, such as worms, woodlice, and ants, help to break down the greens further. When the greens are broken down, the temperature begins to drop and the fungi gets to work on breaking down the browns. Slugs, snails, and beetles also help in this process. Some of the creatures that eat greens also eat mini-beasts, so these are encouraged onto the heap again, all of which helps to break down the compost.

Composting tips

- The nitrogen content (manure is the best source) and type of carbon added determines the quality of the food resources for the microbes. The easier the nitrogen is for the bacteria to use, the faster the bacteria will grow, the more rapidly the temperature will increase, and the hotter the pile will get.

- The particle size of the starting materials is important. The smaller the size of the particles, the easier it is for the bacteria to use the carbon. (Chunky material lets air enter the pile more rapidly, cooling it down and keeping temperatures lower.) Finely chopped material also reduces air pockets in the pile, keeping temperatures higher. However, if the particle size is so small that it promotes very rapid growth, the temperature will increase too quickly and all the oxygen will be used up.

- Carefully selecting the starting materials used controls the internal temperature of the pile and, therefore, the time between turning the heap. The temperature starts at ambient levels, and typically climbs to above 135°F (57°C) in 24–72 hours. If the temperature has not reached that level in that time, something is killing the bacterial biomass. Add more bacteria and more green material to boost the bacterial activity. The temperature should be monitored and remain above 135°F (57°C) throughout the core of the pile—from 1 foot (30 cm) into the heap to the center—with only a short period of reduced temperature each time the pile is turned, for 10 to 15 days. If the temperature doesn't pick up, add more green

material. As the temperature begins to decline (when the oxygen has been used up), it is time to turn the pile again and let in more oxygen. Turning the pile speeds up the time taken to get finished compost, but it is quite possible to build a static compost pile that requires no turning. It will just take longer to break down and may need to be screened to eliminate large chunks, which, incidentally, make great microbial "starters" for the next pile.

- Adequate moisture is vital to let the organisms grow, but as the water content increases above 25 percent, oxygen diffusion is reduced and may lead to anaerobic conditions. Take a handful of compost and check that it's as wet as a wrung-out sponge. Anaerobic bacteria produce toxic alcohols, phenols, and terpines, as well as objectionable odors. If the mix is off, it will smell of rotten eggs or soggy diapers. A healthy compost pile should smell rich and earthy, and be dark and crumbly in texture.

Compost tea

Extracts of compost in water contain as much as 80 percent of the beneficial organisms present in compost, and can be applied to plants in areas difficult or impossible to mulch as normal. Good compost tea can be made in a bucket with a mesh bag of compost suspended in it for 12–24 hours. The critical factor is keeping the liquid aerated. Air bubblers used in aquariums are a good idea, but be sure that the bubbles spread out as they rise. Give

the solution a stir now and then and, *voilà*, you've brewed a potent potion guaranteed to give new life to your soil. Used as a soil drench, compost tea boosts the beneficial bacterial and fungal populations that break down organic matter for use by plants. As a foliar spray, compost tea has actually been shown to create a film of pathogen-resistant organisms that can fight off diseases such as powdery mildew and rust.

WORM COMPOSTING

If there's not much space to devote to compost heaps, vermiculture (worm composting) can be accomplished in very small spaces. Bins, such as the plastic storage bins readily available at any home improvement center, can be modified and used to foster red worms (*Eisenia foetida*). These utilize all the vegetable scraps from the kitchen, eventually returning those organic materials to the kitchen garden soil. Furnish the bin with some starting material, such as good-quality compost, or even shredded newspaper. Then bury the kitchen scraps in this to provide food for the worms.

Irrigation

In general, the goal is to supply the entire field uniformly with water, so that each plant has the amount of water it needs—neither too much nor too little.

Soil types

There are three basic types of soil, and identifying which one you have will dictate many irrigation decisions. At one end of the spectrum is sandy soil, mainly composed of relatively large mineral particles, which allows water to percolate downward through it quickly. In practical terms this means that the water is available to the plants for a much shorter period of time than in denser soils. At the other end of the scale is clay with its much smaller particles that bind tightly together. The main danger is that water is more likely to run off the surface than reach the bottom of the root zone, unless it is applied carefully. This particularly applies in hot, dry summers when the clay surface forms a hard crust. In between is the ideal soil type, loam, and most soils fall somewhere in this middle range. Different amounts of water are needed for each of these three soil types.

Watering your garden

  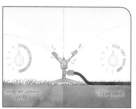  

1 Whatever your soil type, it is best to take a soil sample just before watering to see how damp it actually is. Dig down with a shovel or trowel, or use a probe to pull up a core to inspect. The soil should never be bone dry, nor should it be so wet that you can squeeze moisture out of it. When it's on the dry side, it's time to water; when on the soggy side, wait a few days and try again.

2 Turn on the sprinkler (or irrigation system) and see how long it can run before the water starts to create puddles in the soil. If it's only a few minutes, then the soil is probably more claylike. The other possibility is that it has become hydrophilic (water repellant) through compaction and/or lack of organic content, in which case the next step in the test will reveal if any water is penetrating or not.

3 Re-test the soil after a couple of hours and see how deep the water has penetrated. Generally, 1 inch (2.5 cm) of water will penetrate sandy soil to about 12 inches (30 cm), loam to a depth of 7 inches (18 cm), and clay to just 4–5 inches (10–13 cm). (Most plants, even large trees, have the majority of their roots in the top 12–18 inches (30–45 cm) of soil.)

4 Based on the depth of soil that the water penetrated, you can calculate appropriate watering. Water every 5–10 days: sandy and loamy soils for 20–30 minutes, and clay soils for the same total amount of time in several 5-minute intervals spread out over several hours. Keep checking the moisture of the soil and the health of plants in the garden.

5 You can measure how much water is being applied if you use a sprinkler. Stand several straight-sided containers in the garden to catch the spray. Measure the total volume of water collected after 15 minutes. Multiply that figure by four for the amount of hourly water delivery. If you stand out several containers in a line, at increasing distances from your sprinkler, you can see if you are getting even coverage.

FINDING OUT YOUR SOIL TYPE
Simple observation will help you
assess the type of soil you have and
indicate the right watering regimen.
Dig up a small handful of soil, hold it in
your hand, and press it into a ball.
• The soil is sandy if it falls apart immediately after being released. Sandy
soils will therefore need to be watered
more frequently than loamy soil.
• Loamy soil clumps together but will
crumble with a little prodding.
• Clay sticks to itself like glue and
takes on the shape into which it is
molded. This type of soil benefits from
several short sessions of watering
separated by longer intervals to let the
water percolate down and so reduce
any runoff.

Choosing an irrigation system

For small gardens, hoses and sprinklers are fine. If you have a large area to water—perhaps with several zones that have different water needs—or you just want to fine-tune your watering for increased water efficiency, designing an underground sprinkler or drip system may be to your (and your garden's) advantage. But which does what, and which is best for a given situation?

Sprinklers

Sprinklers use high water pressure and a high volume to deliver water over a large area. Large flower or vegetable beds are prime candidates for rigid sprinkler systems, and a typical system will be plumbed into the water line with its own shut-off valve and sprinkler heads spaced along a buried pipe that will provide complete coverage of the area. The system may also have one or more control valves, with a backflow prevention device, and be wired into an electronic controller.

Sprinkler heads

There are two types of sprinkler head—spray heads and rotary heads:

- Spray heads can cover part of—or a whole—circle, usually with a radius of up to 15 feet (4.5 m). Multiple spray heads are usually installed to overlap and provide complete coverage.
- Rotary heads, which can be either gear-driven or the impact type, can cover a much wider area than spray heads—up to three times their radius—and deliver the water at a slower rate as they sweep the area. This may help prevent "puddling," as the water has a longer time to be absorbed before the next wave.

Drip systems

These dispense lower volumes of water at low pressure through flexible tubing as opposed to a wider, rigid pipe. The connection to the water line is with a rigid pipe and shut-off valve. It will have a control valve with a back-flow cutoff. Since the system uses small-diameter tubes and the emitters themselves have small holes and operate under low pressure, there's an added pressure regulator and an in-line filter. The flexible tubing then snakes through the garden punctuated by emitters that release water directly into the soil (drip by drip) at the base of each plant.

Alternatively, mini- or micro-spray heads can be attached to the ½-inch (12-mm) delivery tubing by even smaller ¼-inch (6-mm) tubes. The final component is a flush valve that allows you to drain or flush the system to clean it out. Besides saving a lot of water, drip systems are very easy to modify. On the downside, the drip irrigation is not the best system for keeping your mulch layers actively decomposing and nutrients evenly cycling. (Mini-sprays do a better job.)

Controlling your irrigation system

Many busy gardeners find that automatic control of their irrigation system is a "must." There are lots of choices, from low-tech wind-up timers to computerized controllers capable of handling multiple zones and cycles. The key to all of these time-saving devices is reassessing their programs frequently as the weather conditions change. They are only as good as their human programmers. Some can be fitted with soil probes and rain sensors to improve their water efficiency. Visit your local nursery, hardware, or irrigation supply store to see the many features and options. Don't be afraid to ask questions; helpful and knowledgeable staff are usually more than happy to help out. If you need extra help, there are many qualified professionals to help you design, install, and/or maintain an irrigation system.

Pests

Gardeners have always been among the more environmentally conscious groups of society, but now more than ever most gardeners are thinking seriously about using nonharmful methods of pest control. As we have learned more about insects, we have begun to reject the "only good bug is a dead bug" mentality and to see some as beneficial in the fight against crop destruction.

As plants put on new growth, there are many pests waiting to strike. Some of the most damaging, such as aphids, pierce the plant tissues with their mouth parts and suck out the sap, the lifeblood of the plant. Other pests, such as slugs and snails, scrape the leaves and stems, leaving big holes or cut all the way across, decapitating them. Various moths lay their eggs on plants so that their caterpillar larvae will have food to eat when they hatch. Instead of using toxic chemicals to control them and render your harvest poisonous, there are many mechanical and nontoxic methods to control them.

Whitefly and mealybug

Other sucking insects that can cause damage include the whitefly and mealybug. An attack by one of these insects reduces plant vitality, causes premature leaf drop, and may result in the demise of your favorite plant.
There are several methods of dealing with them:

- Wash off the eggs and larvae with water or, if they make large colonies, use a horticultural soap solution.
- They are also attracted to, and can be captured by, sticky cards and traps (see the next section for parasitic insects to help in that battle).

Aphids

Aphids transmit plant viruses, cause stunting and deformities of leaves and stems. The first aphids usually appear just when new leaves and flower buds are at their tenderest and most vulnerable, and before their natural predators arrive in sufficient numbers to tackle them.
There are many ways of dealing with aphids:

- For an easy and safe solution, blast them off with a hose.
- Spray them with liquid soap.
- Attract the beneficials to help, such as lady-bugs, hoverflies, and lacewings, by growing flowers such as marigolds in the vicinity.
- Encourage blue tits and other insect-eating birds to the garden by putting up boxes for them to nest in.
- Consider leaving a few select plants to serve as bait for these sap-sucking bugs. One of their favorites is wild lettuce (*Lactuca serriola*), a bristly leaved plant that makes dandelion-

like flowers on top of hollow stems. You may recognize it by the milky sap it bleeds when you break it off in an unsuccessful attempt to pull it out by the roots. Allow the aphids to colonize the wild lettuce, and then pull out the whole plant to dispose of both weed and pest.
- Aphids are also attracted to the color yellow, and yellow sticky cards should be available in your local garden center to attract them to their doom.
- For hardened gardeners and the unsqueamish, however, simply rub aphids out between thumb and forefinger.

Monitor your plants often and get aphids under control before they suck the life out of the tender little buds. You'll find it much easier to wipe out a small, early infestation than a larger one later on.

APHIDS

Aphids feed by sucking up plant juices through a food channel in their beaks. Plant phloem contains lots of sugar but not much nitrogen. To obtain enough nitrogen, aphids must ingest far more sugar and liquid than they actually need. They have special filters in their digestive system to help excrete the excess sugar water consumed, and this coats the plant. Some species of ants are attracted to this and will protect the aphids from natural enemies, carrying them to new plants when the food source is depleted. Some ants even build small shelters for the aphids.

Ants

An increase in aphid, scale, and mealybug populations may also mean an increase in the ants that round them up and harvest their sweet exudates. Here are some methods for going after the ants to keep the aphids at bay:

- In early summer, flood their nests with water to encourage them to move elsewhere.
- Protect pots by smearing petroleum jelly around the sides.
- Use a borax solution to control them.

Borax ant eradicator

1 cup sugar

3 cups water

1 tbsp boric acid powder

1 Boil the water and sugar until the sugar is dissolved. While still hot, stir in the boric acid until all the powder has dissolved. Soak cotton balls in the solution and place them in small jar lids or old film containers.

2 Place in middle of an ant trail. The ants will take the sugar solution back to the nest and eventually will be poisoned.

Note: Keep away from pets and children.

Cabbage loopers

Cabbage loopers are moths that lay their eggs on all cabbage relatives, and the hatching caterpillars can do a lot of damage very quickly. Watch the leaves for holes and fine black droppings to detect their presence. Spray with Bt (*Bacillus thuringiensis*). This natural bacterial enemy will not harm pets or humans, though it will affect butterflies and moths, so use it judiciously.

Slugs and snails

Slugs and snails are nearly ubiquitous, so keep a close eye out for any damage to your plants. With slugs, the tiny gray ones do the most damage, whereas the large black ones live on dead organic matter. Here are some ways of getting rid of slugs and snails:

- Pick them off the leaves as they appear. You could do this by flashlight, as most feed by night.
- You may also uncover a cache of their eggs while digging in your garden. They look like little pearls and, by destroying them, you are getting rid of a whole generation of nasty herbivores.
- An organic bait, made from iron phosphate (never metaldehyde), will kill them without harming anything else.
- Trap the slugs and snails by setting out small dishes of beer among your plants, set level with the soil. Slugs and snails will be attracted to the beer, and they will then drown in it.
- If you have a slug attack in one area in your garden, place a black garbage bag on the ground in between the plants. Put two old lettuce heads inside, add two cups of bran, and pour a cup full of beer over the lettuce. Leave overnight with the top open. The slugs should crawl into the bag and you can simply scoop up the bag.

Birds

Birds, although often an asset to a garden, can ruin a crop of fruit very quickly. Protect fruit on trees with bird netting or hang flashing and fluttering Mylar strips or pinwheels to scare them off. Bird netting can also be laid over rows of tender crops.

Rodents

Physical barriers are required to provide protection from rabbits, gophers, moles, and voles. To keep the burrowing rodents from uprooting plants, put the plants inside wire cages when planting, and sink these cages at least 2 feet (60cm) into the ground. Chicken wire is easily formed into cylinders (crimp the bottom firmly shut) or you can buy ready-made cages at the nursery. Low wire mesh fences keep out rabbits.

Beneficial insects

Not all creatures in the garden are pests. Insects obey all the other rules that govern our biosphere, including the dog-eat-dog life cycle where everything is food for something else. So the puzzle is, which insects will prey on the ones we don't want in our gardens, and how can we attract them? In most cases the juvenile stages of an insect are the carnivorous kind. To ensure that these nymphs are around when the pests appear, it is necessary to keep the parent generation in your garden, and to keep it well fed.

Flowers are the solution. They have evolved a myriad of mechanisms to attract insect pollinators, and these same attractions are available to other insects whether they move pollen or not. The first obvious attraction is the pollen. Pollen is a protein-rich package, produced in copious quantities by most species. The strategy is to produce an attractive energy source for the insects. These unwitting beasts eat a large percentage of the pollen and deposit some of the excess. Another major insect attractant is nectar, a liquid refreshment and pick-me-up that is essentially sugar water. Tiny flies and wasps lay their eggs either on the host plant or even on its pests, including aphids. When the eggs hatch, out come very hungry juveniles whose preferred food just happens to be the very pest you are trying to outwit. Our job is to plant intelligently, fostering the throngs of beneficial insects that would normally occur in a balanced ecosystem.

Planting intelligently

Accessible nectar sources can be found in many plant families, such as sage (lavender, mint, and thyme), mallow (hibiscus, abutilon, and hollyhock), and rose (strawberry, cotoneaster, apples, and blackberries) to name just a few families. Some of those that have extra floral nectaries (nectaries that are not enclosed within the flower) are the euphorbia and pea (lupine, sweet pea, acacia, and wisteria) families. Passion vines also have nectaries on their stems at the base of the leaves. It's important that you plant lots of different kinds of flowers that will bloom at different times of the year to ensure a constant supply of readily available food to a diverse world of insects. And never resort to pesticides, because they'll also kill beneficial insects.

Herbs

Growing your own herbs means that you can select the best varieties, concentrating on your favorites, knowing they'll be packed with fresh flavor and will enliven any meal. You can also guarantee that they won't have been sprayed with anything toxic.

Herbs thrive in pots and containers, providing wonderfully fresh leaves for cooking.

Growing your own plants is not only fun but more economical than buying a small quantity of herbs with a short shelf life in a plastic pouch at a supermarket. It means that you can cut what you want, when you want, and that it is just a matter of minutes from picking to the pot. Having your own herb collection also means you are much more likely to try experimenting with different combinations than when you buy a couple of herbs to order for just one particular recipe.

Scrambled eggs, for example, can easily become a tasty omelet by folding in shredded parsley, sage, rosemary, and thyme. Packaged soups and sauces take on new life when aromatic dill, oregano, or basil is stirred in just before serving. A soothing herbal tisane of lemon balm leaves can be quickly prepared by steeping a few leaves in a cup of boiling water. And what would a mojito be without the pungent, essential oils of fresh mint to complement the bite of the rum?

chervil

Growing herbs

Anyone can grow herbs. They do not require any great skill, and can be raised in containers on the patio or kitchen stoop, on your kitchen windowsill, or in a planter box on the balcony of an apartment. You should have room for a good selection.

Buying young plants

Buying ready-grown plants is the quickest way to start a collection, certainly if you do not have room to grow new plants from seed or cuttings, but you will be limited to the varieties on sale. For the best selection, visit a specialty herb nursery with a choice of say 10 or 15 different kinds of thyme, and perhaps 7 kinds of basil and rosemary, etc. Many mints might be indistinguishable, but other herbs do provide different colors, tastes, and shapes, with some thymes being sprawling spreaders, others striking, upright clumps.

SOWING YOUR SEEDS

Very fine seed is best mixed in a plastic bag with an equal quantity of horticultural sand before sowing. This mix can then be scattered onto the growing medium using a piece of card folded in two, running the seed-and-sand mix down the crease. This will guarantee an even spread of the seed.

Sowing seed

Order specialty catalogs to get the widest choice of seed, and check that you can provide the right growing conditions for the new plants (the two extremes being full sun with quick-draining soil or moist, rich soil in shade for lush growth) before making a final selection. Although you can sow some seed directly outside (always wait until the soil has warmed up and weed seedlings are starting to burst out of the ground), you will invariably get plants off to an earlier start if you grow them indoors on a windowsill or in a heated greenhouse.

1 Fill the container with the growing medium almost to the top. Tap the container to settle the soil, and gently flatten the surface but don't compress it. Moisten with warm water using a fine rose spray.

2 Scatter fine seed evenly across the surface and cover with a thin layer of perlite. For larger seed, insert and cover with perlite. For the largest herb seed, press halfway into the soil.

3 Follow the temperature germination guide on the back of the packet. At this stage warmth is extremely important. If growing in a cupboard, watch for signs of growth and move into light when shoots appear.

4 Cover the tray or put it inside a polythene bag to generate humidity. Remove when the first seedlings appear. Don't place the seedlings in direct sun. Keep in a bright place, and water from below when dry.

5 Transfer seedlings into other containers when large enough to handle. Space well apart to give the roots space. When 2 ½ inches (6 cm) high, transfer to their final pot or bed.

Cuttings

Use established plants (rosemary, chamomile, and thyme) to generate extra plants by taking cuttings. You can take cuttings of new, soft, nonflowering growth in late spring/early summer, greenwood cuttings in the first half of summer, semi-ripe cuttings in late summer, and hardwood cuttings in mid- to late fall, right through the growing season.

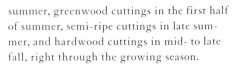

1 Fill a small pot almost to the top with soil mix. Take the cutting of a nonflowering shoot using a sharp knife. Place in a polythene bag and keep shaded.

2 Trim the base of the cutting just below a leaf joint, so it is about 4 inches (10 cm) long. Remove leaves along the bottom third to prevent any unnecessary moisture loss.

3 Dip the cutting in rooting powder. Make a hole in the soil with a dibber and insert the cutting. Firm in place, water, and label. Avoid direct sun and regularly spray with a mister.

4 Once the roots poke through the bottom of the pot, transfer to the next size container. Jumping a size is counterproductive and will not produce a sudden growing spurt.

5 Acclimatize the plant by placing it in a cold frame in dappled shade. When the plant shows good growth, nip out the growing tip to promote plenty of new, bushy growth.

6 When planting out, make sure it is given a weed-free patch of ground. Trim occasionally to create strong, bushy growth and to keep it from becoming too long and leggy.

Where should herbs be grown?

Indoors or out, herbs can either be segregated, kept in a special group, or mixed with annual and perennial flowers. Try tucking a few parsley plants in a container with colorful dahlias, use a creeping form of rosemary to spill out of a potted agave, or combine sage with a drought-tolerant succulent such as hens-and-chicks (*Sempervivum tectorum*). In the garden it is often best to grow herbs in a special area with good access between the narrow beds to make collecting the leaves easier.

HEALTHY ROOTS

To generate a good spread of vigorous roots, plant cuttings in an open, free-draining soil mix. Add a handful of horticultural grit to the medium—this will help the water sluice away. The more quickly water pours through the mix, the more the plant's roots have to forage for moisture. Plants with an extensive root system thrive better than those with a few, wispy growths. If the soil mix is heavy and stays wet, there is a danger that the plant might rot.

Preserving herbs

It is always worth taking extra cuttings to dry or freeze so that you've always got a spare supply of tasty herbs for the kitchen, especially out of season when the garden has died down.

THE BEST PLACES FOR DRYING

Use an oven, which must be at a low temperature, with the door left open. Keep checking to make sure the herbs don't burn. Alternatively try an airing cupboard, or a darkened room, again with the door open for good ventilation. You can use a microwave, but first experiment with small batches of herbs to find the correct time setting. Reckon on 1 minute for small leaves, and 3 minutes for the largest.

When to pick

The best leaf-picking time is just before the plants are about to flower. Remove whole new stems with plenty of healthy, unblemished leaves (do not pick old woody growth or individual leaves), and make sure that the plant's shape stays symmetrical and does not end up lopsided. If the cuttings are wet, quickly pat them dry. From now on you have to work quite quickly. The longer the cuttings are left, the more quickly their flavor diminishes.

Drying

First, wipe the leaves clean if they're covered in soil. Next, remove the moisture gradually (not by a sudden blast of heat) so as to preserve the essential oils. There are several drying methods, but you should always

- Segregate the different herbs into separate batches to avoid confusion and tainting when strongly flavored herbs are next to weaker ones, and because they'll dry at different rates.
- Scatter them in a single layer on a wire or wooden rack, and keep turning them over while drying.

- Place in a dry place, at about 175°F (80°C). The total drying time will vary—depending on the leaves' thickness and the temperature—from four days to a couple of weeks.
- Ensure good ventilation to speed up the process.
- Use a dark place to preserve the herb's color.

You will know when the leaves are ready because they will be completely dry and fragile. Do not be tempted to over-dry them so that they instantly crumble and disintegrate on contact.

Storing

Store in a labeled glass jar with an airtight lid in a dark, warm place. Keep checking for condensation—in which case immediately remove the leaves and redry—and mold.

The faster they are used the stronger the flavor (and dried herbs are approximately three times more powerful than fresh ones). Keep for a maximum of one year, ideally using them over winter. When removing the leaves keep them whole, crushing only when sprinkling into a cooking pot.

Freezing

Fast and easy, freezing herbs is one of the most popular methods, and is ideal for the likes of chives, fennel, parsley, and tarragon with quite delicate leaves. The key steps involve

- Rinsing, if necessary, then shaking dry—but do not pat them, to avoid bruising.
- Putting small amounts of the same herb (unless you are making a bouquet garni) into plastic bags, then labeling.
- Storing in a freezer. Put the bags in a sturdy container so that they do not get crushed by other items.
- Using straight from the bag when cooking.
- Alternatively, chop up the herbs and freeze as ice cubes with ½ ounce (15 g) of herbs to ½ fluid ounce (15 ml) of water in each compartment.

Herb oils

Herb oils (using basil, dill, fennel, marjoram, mint, rosemary, thyme) are an excellent standby over winter. Lightly tap the leaves, mixed with a small amount of olive or sunflower oil, in a pestle and mortar to release the herbs' essential oils. Then pour into a glass container with more oil and screw on the lid. Give the occasional shake and, after two weeks maximum, strain through muslin into a clean glass container. Seal and label. Use on salads, or for sauces and frying.

Using herbs

Use herbs to complement, rather than hide, the flavor of a dish. As we have become increasingly conscious of the quantity of salt and fat in our diets, we can use herbs to counteract the loss of flavor from a favorite recipe.

Making a bouquet garni

Bouquet garni is a French herbal mixture. It consists of a collection of herbs, gathered together and tied into a bundle or sachet in cheesecloth. It is used to enhance the flavor of casseroles, soups, and stocks. There are two versions—a dried version and a fresh version.

Fresh version:
1. Gather together 3 sprigs of parsley, 2 sprigs of thyme, and 1 bay leaf, making sure they have long stems.
2. Tie the bunch together with kitchen string and leave a tail that you can use to pull the bunch in and out of your saucepan. Remove the bundle before serving.

Dried version:
1. Mix together 1 tablespoon parsley, 1 teaspoon thyme, and 1 bay leaf.
2. Wrap the herbs in cheesecloth and tie with kitchen string, again leaving some length for pulling it in and out of the saucepan. Remove the bundle before serving.

Variations: You can vary the mixture of herbs to create different flavors depending on what you are cooking—it would work well to include some rosemary if you are adding your bouquet garni to a lamb stew for example. You could also add a curl of lemon or orange peel to add a citrus punch.

Making pesto

A fresh pesto sauce is one of the simplest and tastiest pasta sauces—it's easy to make, and tastes much better using your fresh herbs straight from the garden.
Makes about 1 cup
- I large bunch basil, washed and dried
- 1 clove garlic
- 1 small handful raw pine nuts
- ¾ cup Parmesan, freshly grated
- 3 tbsp olive oil
- Salt

Put all the ingredients except the oil and salt into a food processor or blender. Whiz for a second or two, then add the oil and a little salt. Taste and correct seasoning.

Variations: Try replacing the basil with equal quantities of watercress, parsley, or arugula to get slightly different tastes.

Fresh vs Dried

A general rule of thumb if substituting fresh herbs for dried herbs is using a ratio of 1 to 3—1 teaspoon of dried herbs to 3 teaspoons of fresh herbs. Dried herbs are very convenient and can be great for longer cooking times, but they don't generally have the same pure flavor as fresh herbs and they can go stale quickly. When substituting, you'll often be more successful substituting fresh herbs for dried herbs, rather than the other way around. Certain recipes, such as pesto, or tomato, mozzarella, and basil salad, rely on using fresh herbs as the main ingredient—the dried variety really would not work. Other recipes may be enhanced by using fresh herbs but you could still get similar results using a dried version—a salad dressing where the dried herbs are left to infuse is a good example. Ginger is an exception to this rule—if a recipe calls for fresh ginger, you cannot substitute ground, as the flavors are completely different. You can perk up the flavor of dried herbs by combining it with some fresh parsley.

Herb teas

Herbs can sometimes act as great medicines and have strong restorative powers. The perfect way to make the most of their abilities is by using fresh herbs from your garden to make herbal teas. Here is a basic method:

● Bring a cup of water to a boil and add your chosen herbs (generally 2 tablespoons of fresh herbs or 1 teaspoon of dried herbs). Cover and leave the herbs to steep. The amount of time to leave the tea to infuse depends on the herbs used—it really is a case of trial and error. Some herbs will begin to taste bitter if left too long. Taste the tea intermittently to gauge how long it should be left. Strain the herbs before drinking.

● Alternatively, place your chosen herbs in a saucepan of cold water and slowly bring to the boil. As soon as the water reaches boiling point, take it off the heat, strain, and enjoy.

Which herbs to use:

Mint—eases stomach and digestive problems, helps relieve headaches, and is relaxing.

Borage—stress relief, relaxation, and calming effects.

Fennel—helps bronchitis, digestive problems, and coughs, and destroys germs. It makes a good after-dinner tea. Use crushed or ground seeds.

Lemon balm—will perk you up in the morning, help bloating, gas, bronchial inflammation, high blood pressure, toothache, earache, and headaches. Lemon balm has anti-bacterial and anti-viral properties. Use the leaves. A good combination is lemon balm and fennel.

Thyme—helps bronchitis, coughs, sinuses, nose and throat, larynx, and whooping cough. It can be used as an anti-bacterial. Thyme tea aids digestion.

Making herbal tea

1. Determine how much tea you will be making.

2. Gently warm your teacups and teapot by running the tap water as hot as possible and filling them with water. Put lids on each to keep in the heat.

3. When the water has come to a rolling boil, empty the teapot of warm water and add the herbal tea leaves/flowers or tea bags. The general rule when making a pot of tea is to add a teaspoon of leaves for each cup and one for the pot. If making tea for only one in a cup or mug, then add the leaves to the mug and pour the boiling water over them.

4. Steep for at least 5 minutes. Although steeping too long can bring out the bitter tannins in black, green, or white teas, herbal teas are different. They generally don't have many tannins and therefore can be steeped anywhere from 5 to 10 minutes. Use extra tea leaves to make a stronger tea, not a longer steeping time.

5. Strain if needed. If you have used loose tea leaves, and don't like leaves floating in your tea, then pour hot tea through the strainer into each cup.

6. Sweeten to taste. Sugar or honey may be used to taste. However, some herbal teas are naturally sweet. Taste each tea by itself first before deciding if milk and honey are needed.

47

Directory

Herbs are a key component of any garden. They add flavor to food, and can be used as an attractive garnish. They are invaluable in cooking, enhancing foods, and enlivening even the simplest meal.

Most herbs can be grown from seed, although for more immediate use you can buy bushes from a garden center. Herbs are particularly satisfying, as they are extremely easy to grow—they can be grown indoors on a sunny windowsill or outdoors in containers or an herb bed. If you are constructing a herb bed, it is best to place it as near to your kitchen as possible for ease of use. This way you will also be able to enjoy their wonderful scents.

Basil and parsley are staple herbs in Western cooking, with cilantro a popular choice in many Eastern dishes. Herbs are an important ingredient in many classic combinations, such as tomato and basil salad, and potatoes and chives. Some herbs have attractive edible flowers or stalks that can be used in cooking. Mint and lemon balm may be infused in boiling water to create soothing drinks, which are wonderful for digestion.

The flavor of fresh herbs is wonderfully intense—when cooking, you will usually need only a small amount, or you may overpower the dish. Deep freezing fresh herbs is a good method to preserve flavor.

Allium schoenoprasum
chives

Leaves, perennial, sun to partial shade, water regularly
- **CUISINE** Useful for fish, potatoes, and soups.
- **GROWING TIPS** Clumps can be cut close to the ground at least three times a year, generating a fresh batch of new growth. Every few years divide and separate large clumps. Potted chives can be moved inside to a bright windowsill for winter harvest. Promptly remove flower stems. Needs rich, moist soil.
- **COOKING TIPS** This onion relative is perfect for adding a mild onion taste to just about anything. Classically used to top baked potatoes and other potato dishes; adds zing to salads and sandwiches.

(Lippia citriodora) Aloysia triphylla
lemon verbena

Leaves, perennial/shrub, full sun, water regularly
- **CUISINE** Lemon verbena leaves are used to add a lemony flavor to fish and poultry dishes, vegetable marinades, salad dressings, jams, puddings, and beverages.
- **GROWING TIPS** Best started from cuttings taken in the late summer, but can also be started from seeds. Pinch out the leaf tips to encourage a bushy plant. New growth doesn't appear until late spring or early summer. Can also be grown in containers placed outdoors during the late spring through summer, and brought indoors once the temperature falls below 20°F (6°C).
- **COOKING TIPS** Both the fresh and the dried leaves can be used in a variety of ways.

Amaranthus spp.
amaranth

Annual, full sun, water regularly

- **VARIETIES** Common names include: Chinese spinach, vegetable amaranth, Joseph's coat, tampala, yin choy (and variations), callaloo (and variations), quelite, quintonil, bledo blanco, chaulai, bhaji, pirum, and namul.
- **CUISINE** Used like spinach and takes on the flavors of whatever cooking process is being employed. In India the leaves add body to curries, and in Middle Eastern countries it may simply be wilted in oil with garlic.

Anethum graveolens
dill

Leaves and seeds, annual, sun, water regularly

- **CUISINE** Traditionally used in German and Scandinavian cuisine.
- **GROWING TIPS** Since it is often a large plant, up to 4 feet (1.25 m) tall, grow it outside in the garden. Harvest leaves as it grows, and then clip the flat-topped flower clusters to use in pickles or wait until dry to gather the seed. Will self-sow if left unharvested. Can cope with free-draining, poor soil.
- **COOKING TIPS** Highly rated with fish dishes, such as salmon. The fresh leaves can also be used as whole sprigs when steaming or braising meats. Chop finely and stir into sauces, add to omelets, or sprinkle over everything from tomatoes to lamb chops. Leaves and seeds are used to flavor vinegar and cucumber pickles.

Angelica archangelica
angelica

Leaves, biennial/perennial, part shade, water regularly

- **CUISINE** The large leaves have a penetrating flavor. Not an essential herb, but well worth its place in an ornamental herb garden.
- **VARIETIES** A. archangelica can hit 8 feet (2.5 m). Also try wild angelica (A. sylvestris) and American angelica (A. atropurpurea), biennials and slightly shorter at 5 feet (1.5 m).
- **GROWING TIPS** Sow in fall in the plant's final position. All are rampant self-seeders.
- **COOKING TIPS** Use young, short, shoots to make candied angelica for decorating cakes. The young leaves can be used when stewing fish and for tossing into a salad, and the seeds are used in sweet pastries.

Anthriscus cerefolium
chervil

Leaves, annual, partial shade, water regularly

- **GROWING TIPS** It grows quickly from seed but bolts quickly in hot weather, so sow in succession every few weeks for a continuous supply. Also makes a good pot plant. Being quite hardy it will provide leaves through winter. Needs light soil. A shady position is best to keep it from flowering (and ruining the leaf taste) too quickly.
- **COOKING TIPS** Use like parsley, to which it has a similar taste, albeit slightly sweeter. Chop fine and add to corn or potato dishes, use to garnish platters of meat or pasta, or tuck sprigs into chicken or fish before baking.

Arctium minus
burdock

Biennial, thistle

- **CUISINE** A stout, handsome plant with large leaves and round heads of purple flowers. The thick, edible taproot has a sweet taste, while the outer husk of the stems can be peeled away. The pith is used like a vegetable. Burdock is known as niubang in China and as gobo in Japan, where it is cooked in soups and stews—classically in kinpira gobo, a soy-braised burdock and carrot dish. Raw burdock has a strong, medicinal taste and smell, but this pungency disappears on cooking. Often paired with dandelion in northern Europe.
- **GROWING TIPS** It will grow in almost any soil, but the roots grow best in light, well-drained soil. The seeds germinate readily and can be sown directly in the earth, in fall or early spring.
- **COOKING TIPS** The leaves can be steamed or sautéed to make a spinach-like dish. The stems can be cooked like asparagus.

Armoracia rusticana
horseradish

Roots, perennial/shrub, full sun, water regularly

- **CUISINE** The roots of this hot, mustard-flavored plant have been used for centuries and are a common accompaniment to roast beef.
- **GROWING TIPS** Horseradish spreads to fill all available space, so use restraint when planting. It is grown by dividing and replanting the root; a piece about 8 inches (20 cm) long is ideal. It likes deep, moist soil but will grow almost anywhere. Dig roots in spring or fall, but for best flavor wait until after the first frosts.
- **COOKING TIPS** Mix small amounts of horseradish with cream, sour cream, yogurt, mayonnaise, or cream cheese and dressings for sauces to serve with meat, fish, and potatoes. It is especially good with beet and smoked trout.

Artemisia dracunculus

tarragon

Leaves, perennial, sun, water moderately

- **CUISINE** Tarragon has a unique, licorice-like flavor. Extremely useful.
- **GROWING TIPS** Plant root divisions or purchased plants in spring. Plants die to the ground in early winter in all zones and sprout again the next spring. Cut stems and strip leaves as early as June, and continue cutting to stimulate new growth throughout the growing season. Fertile, free-draining ground in a sunny hot spot.
- **COOKING TIPS** Use to infuse vinegar and flavor salad dressings, and use in a white sauce for fish or egg dishes. Its flavor can overpower others, so use carefully.

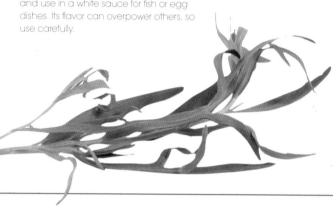

Borago officinalis

borage

Leaves and flowers, annual, sun or shade, average to infrequent watering

- **CUISINE** Borage is used in soups, salads, fruit dishes, and preserves. It is also the main ingredient of a sauce made in Frankfurt, Germany.
- **GROWING TIPS** Give plants plenty of room because they can reach 3 feet (1 m) high and wide. Borage self-sows readily, but seedlings do not transplant well. Either let them grow where they appear or weed out. Needs light, free-draining soil.
- **COOKING TIPS** Generally, only young and tender borage leaves are used because older, tougher leaves are too prickly. The flavor is similar to cucumber, making borage useful in salads or cold soups. Also use in iced tea and fruit drinks.

Carum carvi

caraway

Leaves, roots, and seeds, biennial, sun, water moderately

- **CUISINE** Caraway is native to Northern Africa, the Mediterranean, and much of Europe. It falls into both categories of herb and spice, as it is the seeds that are used primarily, but if you grow it yourself, the leaves and the root are also edible.
- **VARIETIES** It has bright green leaves similar to a carrot top and 18–30-inch (46–75-cm) stems that appear rather weedy-looking. Common varieties include: carvies (Scottish), wild cumin, Roman cumin, and Persian caraway.
- **GROWING TIPS** Caraway does not produce flowers until the second season. Once it does bloom, the flowers are loaded with seeds for drying. Use the leaves as soon as the plant gets big enough to produce enough to meet your cooking or garnish needs. Caraway prefers full sun and a well-drained soil. Harvest seeds before they fall, leaving a few to remain to provide a supply of self-sown seedlings for next year. After harvesting the seeds, cut the entire plant to the ground.
- **COOKING TIPS** The spicy seeds are used in breads (most notably rye bread), pastries, and cheeses.

Chamaemelum

chamomile

Leaves, perennial and annual, full sun or partial shade, Water moderately

- **CUISINE** A soothing, fragrant herb used as a ground covering and in tea.
- **VARIETIES** Two main types of chamomile exist: German Chamomile (*Matricaria recutita*) and Roman Chamomile (*Chamaemelum nobile*).
- **GROWING TIPS** Scatter chamomile seeds and do not cover them with soil. If you start with chamomile plants, plant them in your garden only after the last frost. This herb likes to spread itself (sometimes rather easily), so it doesn't favor containers. Chamomile also enhances the growth of any nearby plants and loves full or partial shade or sun and moist, well-drained earth.
- **COOKING TIPS** Gather the flowers to make the famous chamomile tea. Either variety is fine. The annual, being upright, makes it a bit easier to gather the flower.

Chenopodium ambrosioides

epazote

Perennial or grow as annual; full sun, regular water

- **CUISINE** The leaves of this pungent herb lend a distinctive flavor to Mexican bean dishes. They may also be tucked into a cheese quesadilla for an authentic flavor. Epazote is related to two other food plants, pigweed (also called lamb's quarters) and quinoa.
- **GROWING TIPS** It is easy to cultivate from seed, and may self-sow even in disturbed soils.

Coriandrum sativum

cilantro

Leaves and seeds, annual, sun, water regularly

- **CUISINE** The dried seed is called coriander, and the fresh leaves are called cilantro or Chinese parsley. Both have a pungent flavor that is often married with chilis and other spices in Asian and Latin American food.
- **GROWING TIPS** Sow large batches of seed annually for a fresh crop, then allow several plants to flower and set seed. Tends to bolt quickly in hot weather, and will self-seed if not harvested. Light, free-draining soil.
- **COOKING TIPS** Coriander seeds are generally toasted before being ground to bring out their full flavor. The leaves are used whole, shredded, chopped, or minced.

Cymbopogon citrates

lemon grass

Perennial, full sun, regular water

- **CUISINE** Lemon grass is available as a dried product, but the lemony taste of the fresh stems is definitely superior. It adds a citrus flavor without any acidity to Asian soups and stews and Thai dishes, such as the popular thom ka gai (chicken coconut soup).
- **GROWING TIPS** A warm-climate crop, it can be overwintered in an indoor container. Start from seed or purchase divisions. Harvest the stems by cutting them off at the base. The coarse leaves are tough and have less flavor than the succulent stems.

Foeniculum vulgare

fennel

Stems, leaves and seeds, annual, sun, water regularly.

- **CUISINE** Fennel looks very similar to dill but has tall stalks to 6 feet (2 m) high, and finely cut foliage. Its mildly licorice flavored leaves can be added to fish, fowl, or egg dishes. The seeds are often incorporated into baked food, from bread to cookies.
- **VARIETIES** *F. vulgare azoricum* produces swollen leaf bases that are harvested as a vegetable. Cut off at the ground and trim off the coarse upper stalks and leaves.
- **GROWING TIPS** Sow either variety where it is to grow in the garden. Left uncut, the plants will self-seed. Fertile, free-draining ground.
- **COOKING TIPS** With its subtle anise flavor, the root can be served as a crisp raw vegetable sliced into salads.

Hyssopus officinalis

hyssop

Flowers and leaves, perennial, sun, water moderately

- **CUISINE** Excellent multi-purpose Mediterranean herb that spreads on walls and banks, and can be used (both flowers and leaves) in a wide range of recipes from salads to stuffings.
- **VARIETIES** There is just one species, the semi-evergreen, blue-flowering *H. officinalis*, which also provides *H. o. albus* (white flowers) and *H. o. roseus* (pink), and *H. o. subsp. aristatus*, which is 8 inches (20 cm) shorter than the rest at 2 feet (0.5 m) high.
- **GROWING TIPS** Needs a sheltered, sunny position (ideally at the base of a south-facing wall) in free-draining ground, where it will make a low hedge.

Laurus nobilis

bay

Leaves, evergreen, sun, water moderately

- **CUISINE** From southern Europe, now widely used. Use in soups, stews, and sauces.
- **VARIETIES** *L. nobilis* is the traditional Mediterranean bay, but *Umbellularia californica* has a similar, stronger flavor. Try fresh leaves from *Syzygium polyanthum* (Indonesian laurel), with glossy, dark leaves.
- **GROWING TIPS** Provide quick-draining ground in a sheltered hot spot. In areas with cold, wet winter soil, plants must be grown in containers where they can be given the right soil mix. Can be grown as a mophead, with a ball of leaves on top of a tall vertical or spiraling-up stem.
- **COOKING TIPS** Use fresh leaves sparingly to add a subtle extra flavor to meat and fish dishes.

Levisticum officinale
lovage

Leaves, perennial, sun or part shade, average watering

- **CUISINE** A Mediterranean herb, loved by the ancient Greeks, now scattered widely from North America to Australia. Very useful.
- **VARIETIES** A one-species plant (with no hybrids or cultivars) growing up to 6 feet (2 m) high and 3 feet (1 m) wide after 4 years.
- **GROWING TIPS** Make sure the planting position has plenty of well-rotted compost, because rich, deep soil is vital, as is good drainage. Also provide plenty of room for its impressive growth.
- **COOKING TIPS** Excellent when you need the taste of celery in soups and stews, etc. Also add to salads. Add the crushed seed to bread and pastries.

Melissa officinalis
lemon balm

Leaves, perennial, sun/light shade, water regularly

- **CUISINE** A relative of the true mints, lemon balm has both a mint and a lemony taste. A good herb when you have a spare gap.
- **GROWING TIPS** Lemon balm spreads quickly, so either contain it within the garden or grow in a pot. Propagate from seeds or root divisions. Stem cuttings also root easily. Not fussy about soil.
- **COOKING TIPS** Leaves may be steeped as tea or added to fruit drinks and salads. Lemon balm will also lend interest to custard puddings, soups, and salads.

Mentha spicata
mint

Leaves, perennial, sun/light shade, water regularly

- **CUISINE** Essential.
- **VARIETIES** There are several species and varieties of mint, but when most people say mint, they mean peppermint (*M. piperita*) or spearmint (*M. spicata*). Apple mint is *M. suaveolens*, and the variegated variety is often called pineapple mint; orange bergamot or orange mint is a variety of peppermint (*M. piperita citrata*).
- **GROWING TIPS** Mint spreads rapidly so keep it contained. Grow in a large pot (or bucket) above or sunk below ground. Start from established plants or root divisions. Stem cuttings root easily. Rich, free-draining soil.
- **COOKING TIPS** Mint leaves can be harvested fresh or dried for later use. All varieties lend their fresh flavor to tea (iced or hot), fruit drinks, and vegetables, such as peas and carrots. Mint jelly is a classic lamb accompaniment; chopped mint lends itself to other meat dishes.

Monarda didyma
bergamot

Perennial, sun/light shade, water regularly

- **CUISINE** The colors range from scarlet to white and the scent is similar to the bergamot orange (a citrus fruit used to flavor Earl Grey tea). The flowers are very popular with bees, and it has a flavor reminiscent of cucumber.
- **GROWING TIPS** Bergamot plants like sun or very light shade and thrive on most soils, except very dry or clay. Keep them well watered over summer. It's best to plant bergamots behind smaller plants that will hide the lower part of their stems. They can easily be divided in the spring as they start growing. This rejuvenates tired old clumps and provides plenty of new, vigorous plants. Alternatively, take cuttings when growth is fresh and thriving.
- **COOKING TIPS** The stems can also be used for culinary purposes by cutting them before the bergamot blossoms. Remove the leaves from the stems before storing. Use the dried leaves in herb tea. Use fresh young leaves sparingly in salads, fruit salads, and fruit drinks. The bright blue, star-shaped flowers can be added to drinks and salads, or frozen in ice cubes and added to summer drinks.

Myrrhis odorata
sweet cicely

Leaves, perennial, part shade, water moderately

- **CUISINE** A European herb with leaves tasting of aniseed, and roots that can be eaten raw or cooked like a vegetable. Useful because of its long season, emerging early and dying down late in fall.
- **GROWING TIPS** Promptly remove the flower stalks or the flavor deteriorates. This also stops self-seeding. Cut right back in midsummer, to generate a second batch of fresh leaves. Provide moderately rich, moist soil with good drainage.
- **COOKING TIPS** Try the seeds in fruit salads, ice cream, and apple pie. The leaves perk up soups and stews, and reduce the acidity of gooseberry and rhubarb recipes. Chop the roots into a salad.

Myrtus communis
myrtle

Leaves, fruit, and flowers, perennial/shrub, full sun to partial shade, water regularly

- **CUISINE** Also known as True Myrtle, myrtle is an evergreen shrub or small tree with dense foliage, growing to approximately 10 feet (3 m) high.
- **GROWING TIPS** The plant prefers sandy, loamy, and clay soils and requires well-drained soil. The plant prefers acid, neutral, and alkaline soils. It cannot grow in the shade. It requires dry or moist soil and is highly drought tolerant.
- **COOKING TIPS** The fruit has an aromatic flavor. It can be eaten fresh when ripe or can be dried and then used as an aromatic food flavoring. The leaves are used as a flavoring in cooked savory dishes. The dried fruits and flower buds are used to flavor sauces, syrups, etc. An essential oil from the leaves and twigs is used as a condiment, especially when mixed with other spices. The flowers have a sweet flavor and are used in salads.

Nepeta racemosa
catmint

Leaves and flowers, perennial, partial shade, water regularly

- **CUISINE** A free bloomer whose billowy mounds of lavender, pink, or white flowers are as opulent as its aromatic foliage, having a fragrance of mint and lemon. The lavender-blue varieties are often used as a substitute for lavender plants.
- **VARIETIES** Catmint has slightly aromatic gray-green foliage that has a delicate, lacy appearance. It has a somewhat sprawling growth habit, making it a nice plant for edges—there are a few tall growing varieties, like 'Six Hills Giant', with a more upright habit.
- **GROWING TIPS** Most catmints will re-bloom if sheared back after their initial flowering. Some won't provide much of a second show, but their foliage will be refreshed and tidied by the shearing. Division is not a requirement, but if you'd like more plants, catmint responds well to division in the spring.
- **COOKING TIPS** The leaves are used as a flavoring in food and for their minty lemon aroma.

Ocimum basilicum
basil

Leaves, annual, full sun, water regularly

- **CUISINE** Basil is key in several cuisines, such as Asian and Italian, and its leaves lend a bright, almost licorice-like taste to stir-fries, sauces, salads, pasta, and pizza.
- **GROWING TIPS** Remove any flower stalks or the leaves develop a bitter taste. Harvest individual leaves or remove stems, which helps make bushier plants. Provide free-draining, rich soil in a sunny, sheltered site. Water regularly.

O. basilicum var. hyrsiflora
Thai basil

Annual, full sun, water regularly

- **CUISINE** The selections of this leafy herb that are called 'Siam Queen' or 'Thai Basil' have a particularly strong flavor. They typically have large leaves, allowing them to be used as wrappers for other ingredients.
- **GROWING TIPS** Plant in the ground or grow in containers. Pinch out the tips frequently to encourage branching.

Origanum vulgare
oregano

Leaves, perennial, sun, water moderately.

- **CUISINE** Widely used in Greek and Italian cusines.
- **GROWING TIPS** Make sure you take root cuttings from a well-flavored parent because some kinds may be too mild, or buy seeds or young plants from a reputable nursery. Harvest stems and strip off leaves for immediate use or drying, before they elongate and flower. Free-draining, poor ground.
- **COOKING TIPS** Use it fresh or dried; it is one herb that loses little flavor in the drying process.

Petroselinum crispum
parsley

Leaves, annual, light shade, water regularly.

- **CUISINE** Tends to be favored.
- **VARIETIES** Although parsley is actually a biennial (flowering in its second year), in the kitchen garden it is grown as an annual and harvested for its vitamin-rich leaves. Flat-leaf parsley—also known as Italian—has a stronger taste than the curly-leaf—or French—kind.
- **GROWING TIPS** Seeds may take several weeks to germinate. Soaking seed in warm water for a day before sowing can speed up the process. Parsley is best started where it will grow.

Piper sanctum
hierba santa

Herbaceous shrub, full sun or partial shade, regular water

- **CUISINE** Hailing from the genus of plants that produce black (and other colored) pepper berries, which are the seeds of the plant, it is the leaves of hierba santa that provide a licorice-like flavor to Mexican quesadillas, beans, and stews.
- **GROWING TIPS** The heart-shaped leaves are relatively large, being 6–8 inches (15–20 cm) across. The plant may be pruned to encourage more branching and thus more leaf production. Pick them before they get too old or they may be too tough to eat, although they will still impart their characteristic taste.

Portulaca oleracea
verdolaga

Annual, full sun or partial shade

- **CUISINE** Also called purslane in English-speaking countries and pourpier in French, this succulent herb probably originated in India but has gone on to invade every continent with a suitable climate and is often seen as a weed. Wherever it grows, it is most often eaten raw as a salad, but it can add a tart flavor to a soup or frittata, or be combined with other vegetables. Never cook for more than a few minutes or its succulent stems may turn slimy. Late in the season, the stems may be too tough to eat but the leaves will still be tasty and crisp. In Mexico, a handful of purslane may be dropped into soups or stews, or steamed and served topped with grated cheese.

Rosmarinus officinalis
rosemary

Leaves, shrub, sun, water moderately

- **CUISINE** A highly aromatic shrub originally from the Mediterranean. Its resinous needle-like leaves lend their pungent flavor to meats and sauces.
- **GROWING TIPS** Rosemary is quite drought tolerant, and can survive moderately cold winters with protection. In areas with very cold winters, keep the root zone as dry as possible while dormant. Take tip cuttings in midsummer. Well-drained, slightly alkaline soil.
- **COOKING TIPS** Whole fresh sprigs can be laid on roasting meat, and woody rosemary twigs can even be stripped to use as skewers for grilling vegetables, meat, and fish. Dried leaves also enhance sauces and soups.

Rumex acetosa
sorrel

Leaves, perennial, sun and part shade

- **CUISINE** An excellent extra herb.
- **VARIETIES** The prime candidates are the 4-feet- (1.25-m) high common sorrel (*R. acetosa*) and two shorter kinds, the 9-inch (23-cm) sheep's sorrel (*R. acetosella*) and 18-inch (45-cm) buckler leaf sorrel (*R. scutatus*).
- **GROWING TIPS** Sorrel self-seeds quickly, so cut off the flower heads to avoid a mass of seedlings. To prevent the leaves from becoming bitter in hot summers, add a thick mulch to keep the roots cool and moist. Needs moderate to deep, rich, moist ground and good drainage.
- **COOKING TIPS** Can be used in soups and fish sauces, with meats and salads.

Salvia officinalis
sage

Leaves, perennial/shrub, sun, water moderately

- **CUISINE** A classic herb, the soft, downy leaves lending their characteristic taste to meat dishes and breads. Essential.
- **VARIETIES** There are many varieties, including some variegated ones. The typical gray-green leaves may be bordered with golden yellow (*S. o.* 'Ictarina') or flushed with red violet (*S. o.* 'Purpurascens'), and one has an irregular cream border (*S. o.* 'Tricolor').
- **GROWING TIPS** Snip off the growing tips and strip the leaves to encourage branching and keep the shrub from growing leggy. Free-draining, alkaline soil in sheltered site. Winter protection vital for young plants.
- **COOKING TIPS** Fresh or dried sage can season hearty soups and gravies. Pineapple sage (*S. elegans*) adds an exotic taste to fruit dishes and drinks.

Sanguisorba minor
salad burnet

Leaves, perennial, light shade, water regularly

- **CUISINE** Once popular as a fodder plant, salad burnet is now regarded as a specialty herb. A good backup.
- **GROWING TIPS** Grow salad burnet from seed, sowing about ½ inch (1.5 cm) deep and thinning plants to 12 to 15 inches (30 to 40 cm) apart. Harvest young leaves and remove emerging flower stalks to encourage growth. Self-seeds easily. Average soil, ideally chalky.
- **COOKING TIPS** Dry the leaves quickly to retain as much flavor and color as possible. When dried there's a slightly more nutty flavor. It lends its cucumber flavor and aroma to salads, and to season cream cheese or butter spreads when used fresh.

Satureja
savory

Leaves, annual/perennial, sun

- **CUISINE** Both summer and winter savory have a similar delicate flavor, which is a blend of pepper, marjoram, and thyme.
- **GROWING TIPS** Sow both species from seed, either directly on the surface of the soil or very lightly covered, because it requires good light to germinate. Harvest summer savory leaves from an early stage until the end of the season. Winter savory leaves can be harvested any time during the growing season. Either may be dried if there is a surplus. Free-draining, poor ground.
- **COOKING TIPS** Both types can be added to sauces for fish, or infusing vinegars for salad.

Thymus
thyme

Leaves, perennial/shrub, full sun

- **CUISINE** An essential herb for the kitchen used to enhance the flavor of many different foods and recipes. Most varieties grow to only 6 to 12 inches (15 to 30 cm) in height, and they make an attractive edging for the perennial border.
- **VARIETIES** There are numerous varieties of thyme, divided into two groups, creeping and bush thyme. All are suitable for cooking.
- **GROWING TIPS** Thyme likes a hot sunny spot with good-draining soil. It is planted in the spring and thereafter grows as a perennial. It can be propagated by seed or cuttings, or by dividing rooted sections of the plant. Tolerates drought well. Leaves can be harvested throughout the summer, but flavor is best just before flowering. To dry, cut the stems just as the flowers start to open and hang in small bunches. Harvest sparingly the first year.

Trigonella foenum-graecum
fenugreek

Annual, full sun, regular water

- **CUISINE** Most people know the flavor of fenugreek from its seed, which is a major component of curry powder. In India and Pakistan, fenugreek, when harvested as a young seedling plant, is served as a green vegetable called methi. Fenugreek greens are bitter, but have a celery- and-spinach-like flavor. Because of this, they are often used in conjunction with other vegetables that mellow that quality. Chopped fenugreek is added to bread dough and made into fritters with garbanzo bean flour.
- **GROWING TIPS** Sow the seed in spring and harvest some of the young plants as greens.

Edible flowers

The finishing touch for any dining table is, traditionally, a floral arrangement. But why stop there? It's time to take flowers as far as the plate! An astounding variety of garden blooms are not only suitable for garnishing, but deliciously edible, too.

Gardeners grow many plants for their flowers. Lovely colors and pleasing fragrances are terrific in the garden, but for gourmets, flowers are another way of adding color and taste to a meal. In fact many flowers are not just edible but very tasty. Sweet, spicy, or exotically aromatic, they can be used in many ways.

Most flowers do not stand up to cooking temperatures and are best incorporated at the last minute or used as a garnish.

Using flowers

With their seemingly endless variations of form, color, scent, and texture, flowers offer great culinary potential. Inedible flowers offer decorative flair; edible ones can be eaten warm—including stuffed, battered, or fried—or sprinkled over salads and served cold.

Harvesting and preparation

The best time to harvest edible flowers is in the early morning, after any dew has evaporated. This is when the water content of the blooms is at its highest. Avoid any that are not fully open.

GOLDEN COLORING

The yellow color of marigolds comes from calendulin, a gummy substance contained within the flowers. You can use this natural colorant to add a beautiful golden hue to your food. Try soaking marigold petals in twice their volume of warm milk, until the milk takes on a soft yellow color. Use the milk in your cooking—from breads and cakes to rice puddings and batters for deep-frying.

IMPORTANT DOS AND DON'TS
- Pick only organically grown flowers.
- Don't use flowers from a florist or nursery, as they may have been treated with pesticides unsuitable for food plants.
- Don't eat flowers picked from roadsides.
- Don't eat flowers if you suffer from hay fever or allergies, as pollen may trigger problems.
- Do remove the pistil and stamen from most flowers—except violets, pansies, Johnny-jump-ups, runner bean, and edible pea flowers.

1 To clean the flowers, shake each one to dislodge any insects. Wash the flowers in a strainer placed in a large bowl of water. Add a pinch of salt to the water to get rid of any remaining insects.

2 Drain, then let the flowers dry naturally at room temperature on paper towels. They will retain their color and scent providing they are not exposed to direct sunlight.

3 Remove the pistils, stamens, and any attached sepals from each flower before eating.

4 Separate the flower petals from the rest of the flower just before use, to minimize the risk of wilting. Cut the white base of each petal, as this is often bitter.

Crystallizing flowers

Crystallized flowers make a beautiful garnish for cakes and desserts of all kinds. Violets are most commonly used—but you could substitute any edible flowers, such as lavender, pansies, rose petals, or geraniums. Be sure to pick only flowers that have not been treated with pesticides. Leave the stem intact when picking, and do not wash the flowers, as dampness will make crystallizing impossible.

Begin by beating 1 egg white in a small bowl until it is foamy. Take a violet by the stem and dip it into the egg white. Use a fine paintbrush to spread the egg carefully over every surface of the flower. Use a metal skewer to open the petals and brush the inside surfaces. Now sprinkle all surfaces of the petals with superfine sugar, trim off the stem, and spread the flowers on a metal rack in a warm, dry place to allow them to dry out. Leave them for several days, then test for dryness by checking for spots of moisture in the heart of the flower. Once they are completely dry, place the violets in a cardboard box in layers separated by tissue paper.

Stuffing zucchini flowers

This is an easy recipe that is quick to prepare. It is also an attractive dish that will be a talking point with your guests.

1 Pick 12 zucchini flowers when they are fresh and not yet fully open. Remove the stamen from inside the flower but retain the stem, which you can use to pick up the flower without damaging it. The best stuffing mix to use is a classic Italian mixture of cheese and egg. Mix:
4 oz ricotta
4 tbsp fresh breadcrumbs
4 tbsp freshly grated parmesan cheese
2 beaten eggs
large pinch of freshly grated nutmeg (Once smooth, spoon the mixture into the flowers.)

2 Beat together 1 beaten egg, 2 oz all-purpose flour, and enough cold water to make a smooth, loose batter. Dip the stuffed flowers briefly into the batter and shake off any excess mixture. Heat about 6 tbsp olive oil in a large skillet and fry the flowers in the oil until golden-brown on each side. Drain excess oil from the flowers by placing on paper towel, and serve while still hot.

Lavender sugar

Sugar infused with fragrant lavender is perfect for using in cookie dough, or sprinkling onto cakes or desserts. Cut lavender flowers from the plant, and strip them from the stems. Stir the flowers into a bowl of superfine sugar and place in an airtight container. A good ratio to obtain a delicately scented sugar is 2 tablespoons of lavender per 1 cup sugar. Store in a cool, dry place for 1–2 weeks to allow the flavor to infuse, shaking the container occasionally to distribute the flowers among the sugar. After infusing, sift the sugar to remove the lavender heads and place the sugar back in its airtight container.

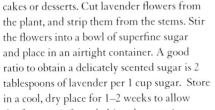

Directory

Edible blooms are to be found in every corner of the garden, from flower-border annuals, such as nasturtiums and marigolds, to perennial favorites, including herbs and other small shrubs, and fruit trees.

Annuals grow from seed to the flowering stage within a single year. Space permitting, sow a row or patch of seed directly in the ground, according to the seed packet directions, or start them off in flats or small pots and transplant them to their final position when they are seedlings. All annuals need sun and regular watering. Harvesting times will vary according to the type of plant and its culinary uses.

Some annuals, such as pretty, heart-shaped pansies, make wonderful garnishes for sweet and savory dishes alike, and can be crystallized and used to adorn festive cakes. Others, such as onion and dill flowers, are suitable only for enhancing the flavor of savory dishes. The flowers of the squash plant are particularly versatile, and are used in Mexican dishes in various ways, including being floated as a garnish on soup.

Many perennial plants have delicious flowers; lavender, rosemary, and fruit trees being good examples, all capable of turning an average plate into something special. The trumpet-shaped blooms of gladiolus and day lilies can be receptacles for stuffings, such as cream cheese or sorbet. Rose petals are used to flavor rose waters and jellies, and desserts can be garnished with fresh or candied fruit blossoms. Frozen in ice cubes, made into teas and wines, or used for flavoring vinegars, marinades, and dressings, the potential for edible flowers goes on and on.

Allium spp.
onion, garlic

Biennials from seed or annuals from sets, sun or partial shade, regular water

- **CUISINE** Usually grown for their flavorful corms or bulbs, their flowers are also edible.
- **GROWING TIPS** Even if the main harvest is for their underground parts, leave some to mature and bloom. The flowers are small and occur in large umbels, and are white or pinkish.
- **COOKING TIPS** The flavor is reminiscent of the bulb, but milder. Use in salads. Flowers from 80–100 days from sets, and 125–175 days from seed.

Anethum graveolens
dill

Annual, sun, regular water

- **CUISINE** All parts of the plant have the characteristic flavor that goes so well with seafood and root vegetables.
- **COOKING TIPS** The cream-white to yellow flowers are held on a large umbel and can be stirred into salad dressings, dips, and hot or cold soups. The flavor is slightly stronger than that of the leaves.

Begonia spp. and cultivars

begonia

Perennials or treat as annuals or grow under glass, shade, regular water

- **CUISINE** Sweet but tart, the small white, pink, or red flowers of species begonias add a crunchy tang to fruit salads. The brightly colored petals of tuberous begonias can also be tossed with other greens or used to garnish complementary foods.
- **GROWING TIPS** All begonias are frost-tender, but many make excellent house-plants and will bloom if given enough light. Keep moist in rich soil.

Borago officinalis

borage

Annual, sun or partial shade, low water

- **CUISINE** The young leaves lend a cucumber-like flavor to salads and cooked greens.
- **GROWING TIPS** The sky-blue flowers are popular with bees and humans.
- **COOKING TIPS** Float the flowers in cool drinks, such as lemonade or fruit punch. They are also tasty in chilled soups like vichyssoise.

Calendula officinalis

marigold

Annual, sun, regular water

- **CUISINE** Flavors range from spicy to bitter, tangy to peppery. The taste resembles saffron but is more pungent.
- **COOKING TIPS** Sprinkle them on soups, pasta or rice dishes, herb butters, and salads. Petals add a yellow tint to soups, spreads, and to scrambled eggs.

Chrysanthemum coronarium

edible chrysanthemum

Annual, full sun or partial shade, regular water

- **CUISINE** Although the edible chrysanthemum is native to the Mediterranean, it has become a fixture in Asian cuisine. In Japan it is called *shungiku* in spring and *kikuna* in the fall. It is served in soups and sukiyaki, or is boiled to remove its bitterness and served as a vegetable or condiment. Avoid overcooking, as it becomes an unattractive mush if added to a dish too soon. It also features in a complex Korean condiment with soy sauce, sesame oil, scallion, garlic paste, toasted sesame seeds, pepper, rice vinegar, and sugar. The stems and leaves are usually used, but the flower petals can also be included.
- **GROWING TIPS** This chrysanthemum flowers in late summer, but should be harvested for its greens before temperatures get near 80°F (27°C). They are unpalatably bitter in the heat. Sow the seed when the soil is warm.

Crocus sativus

saffron

Full sun, regular water

- **CUISINE** Saffron has been highly esteemed for thousands of years. Its spread through central Asia and around the Gulf of Arabia has fostered a variety of interesting dishes that feature its distinctive aroma and flavor. The rose-purple flowers are not particularly showy, but the brilliant orange stigma is the prize. It takes a dozen or so flowers to provide the seasoning for just one batch of paella or bouillabaisse. Pluck the stigmas as soon as the flowers open, and dry them for later use.

- **GROWING TIPS** Since the plant is sterile (and produces no seeds), it must be propagated by division. It's no wonder, then, that it is the most expensive spice. There is no good substitute: Fortunately it is highly aromatic and just a little can go a long way. Plant the corms 2–3 inches (5–7.5 cm) deep and 3–4 inches (7.5–10 cm) apart when available. Saffron will flower in fall before the foliage appears. The corms require a dormant period over summer, which must be dry. Divide the corms and re-plant after the foliage dies down.

Cucurbita pepo
squash

Annual, sun, regular water

- **CUISINE** The flowers are used in many Mexican dishes. They are folded into cheese quesadillas, floated on vegetable soups, and stuffed with various fillings, battered, and fried. Other cultures also use them, and stuffed squash blossoms and baby squashes with the flower attached appear on various restaurant menus.

- **GROWING TIPS** Use only the male flowers if you don't want to limit production of the squashes. The female flowers have a visible swelling between the flower and stem that develops into the fruit. Pick the flowers early in the day when they first open, and before pollinating insects have a chance to arrive. Pinch out the stamens before using.

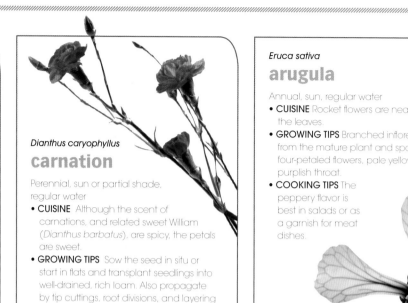

Dianthus caryophyllus
carnation

Perennial, sun or partial shade, regular water

- **CUISINE** Although the scent of carnations, and related sweet William (*Dianthus barbatus*), are spicy, the petals are sweet.
- **GROWING TIPS** Sow the seed in situ or start in flats and transplant seedlings into well-drained, rich loam. Also propagate by tip cuttings, root divisions, and layering established plants.
- **COOKING TIPS** Use flowers whole to garnish desserts or steep in wine to impart their flavor. Cut petals away from the bitter base and use in salads, jellied desserts, or sauces.

Fuchsia hybrids
fuchsia

Woody perennials, shade, regular water

- **CUISINE** The showy flowers have quite a bland taste but make delightful decorations on food dishes.
- **GROWING TIPS** Plants are frost-tender, but thrive in pots in conservatories and bay windows.
- **COOKING TIPS** Remove the stamens and stigma and fill with jam to serve with muffins and toast, or with cream to garnish cakes.

Eruca sativa
arugula

Annual, sun, regular water

- **CUISINE** Rocket flowers are nearly as spicy as the leaves.
- **GROWING TIPS** Branched inflorescences rise from the mature plant and sport small, four-petaled flowers, pale yellow with a purplish throat.
- **COOKING TIPS** The peppery flavor is best in salads or as a garnish for meat dishes.

Gardenia jasminoides
gardenia

Woody perennial, shade, moist soil

- **CUISINE** Dried gardenia flowers impart their floral fragrance to jasmine tea.
- **GROWING TIPS** Gardenias require warmth, good drainage, and consistent moisture. Grow in protected spots in the garden or in pots under glass.
- **COOKING TIPS** Float fresh flowers in punch bowls or use to garnish other fruit dishes.

Gladiolus spp. and hybrids

gladiolus

Perennial corms, sun, regular water

- **CUISINE** Almost any shade of the rainbow can be had from a gladiolus flower, and some even have stunning throat decorations and striations at the edge. The mild flowers are useful as a garnish or when tossed in salad.
- **GROWING TIPS** Grow the corms in rich, well-drained soil after it has warmed up. Plant at a depth twice that of the corm to encourage strong stems, though they may still need staking to keep the larger flowering forms vertical.
- **COOKING TIPS** Stuff the flowers with cream cheese and serve with bread.

Helianthus annuus

sunflower

Annual, sun, regular water

- **CUISINE** When mature, sunflowers are covered with rough hairs and are unpalatable, but the immature flower buds are tender and may be steamed or fried, tasting like an artichoke (another member of this family). The petals (actually individual flowers) can be used as colorful and pungent additions to salads and soups.
- **GROWING TIPS** The diversity of sunflower varieties is growing rapidly. Besides the classic tall, single-stemmed kind there are shorter-stemmed ones, and some that branch, making them ideal for cut flowers.

Hemerocallis cultivars

daylily

Perennials, sun or partial shade, regular water

- **CUISINE** Daylily petals are sweet and crisp with a slight melon-like flavor.
- **GROWING TIPS** Plant root divisions in almost any soil type. Plants are quite drought tolerant and resist most pests.
- **COOKING TIPS** Use whole flowers as decoration on fruit and cheese plates, or toss petals in salads. The trumpet-shaped flowers can also be filled with softened sorbet or ice cream, and frozen for desserts.

Hibiscus spp. and hybrids

hibiscus annuals

Perennials, and shrubs, sun, varies by species

- **VARIETIES** Rose of Sharon or Chinese hibiscus (*H. syriacus*) is a deciduous shrub, rose mallow (*H. moscheutos*) a perennial, and tropical hibiscus (*H. rosa-sinensis*) an evergreen shrub.
- **CUISINE** All have the distinctive mallow flowers with a pinwheel of showy petals surrounding the stamens and stigma. All are also edible and highly ornamental in the garden and on the table.
- **COOKING TIPS** Use as a garnish or stuff individual flowers with savory or sweet cheese balls. Individual petals may be sugared by dipping them in syrup, coating with superfine sugar, and drying to create stained-glass-like decorations.

Lavandula spp.

lavender

Woody perennials, sun, drought tolerant

- **CUISINE** The flowers carry the majority of its essential oils, so these tiny purple flowers can be added to teas and punches to impart a soothing quality. Queen Elizabeth I apparently had lavender conserve made for her private use;
- **COOKING TIPS** Lavender flowers can be steeped in vinegar to make a pleasant dressing for fruits and greens.

Malus spp., *Pyrus* spp., and *Prunus persica*

apple, pear, and peach

Deciduous trees, sun, regular water

- **CUISINE** Sweetly aromatic, the flowers of these fruit trees are also edible.
- **GROWING TIPS** Select varieties that correspond to your climate zone, and plant bare-root trees when the frosts have finished, but before the leaves have begun to appear.
- **COOKING TIPS** Garnish desserts with fresh blossom, or candy them by dipping in syrup, coating with superfine sugar and allowing to dry.

Phaseolus coccineus

scarlet runner bean

Perennial, sun, regular

- **CUISINE** These bright red bean flowers perk up any dish. Having little to no flavor makes them the ideal garnish for many recipes.

Pisum sativum

edible pea

Annual, sun, regular water

- **CUISINE** It may be hard to sacrifice the pea flowers knowing that you are losing succulent peas, but if you have a surplus, try eating the delicate, pale flowers. They are slightly sweet and crunchy, and they taste like peas.
- **COOKING TIPS** Add the flowers to salads, sandwiches, and garnishes.

Rosa spp.

rose

Woody perennials, sun, regular water

- **CUISINE** Rose petals are known for their lovely fragrance. This also blends well with sweet and savory dishes. Rose hips are the fruit of the rose plant, consisting of several dry fruitlets enclosed by the enlarged, fleshy, usually red floral cup that is used for jelly or tea.
- **COOKING TIPS** Rose jelly and rose water are well known, but rose petals can also be used to flavor cream cheese. Rose hips need sweetening but make great jams and jellies and are a great source of vitamin C.

Taraxacum officinale

dandelion

Perennial, sun, regular water

- **CUISINE** The dandelion is a member of the daisy family and is also quite close in relation to chicory. The sunshine yellow flowers have a sweet, honey-like flavor and are sweetest when picked young. The leaves have the highest vitamin A content of all greens.
- **GROWING TIPS** Dandelion requires a long growing season and develops best at low temperatures. Sow seeds ¼ to ½ inch (5 mm–1 cm) deep in late spring to early summer and thin seedlings to 8 to 12 inches (20–30 cm) apart in the row. Harvest in the fall when plants are of satisfactory size. Cut just below the crown with a sharp knife so that the leaves remain attached. Unharvested plants may be left for use in the following spring.
- **COOKING TIPS** The young leaves of the dandelion are best served simply steamed or tossed in salads. They can also be used to make wine, and the root can be ground and used as a coffee substitute.

Tropaeleum majus

nasturtium

Annual, sun or part shade, regular water

- **VARIETIES** Garden nasturtiums come in a wonderful array of colors from near white to deepest burgundy red; many have orange streaks in the throat.
- **CUISINE** All parts of the plant are edible, and the leaves and flowers make peppery additions to salads.
- **COOKING TIPS** The flowers are the perfect garnish for meat and cheese, and can also be used as small cups for savory fillings, such as salmon mousse. Immature seed pods can be pickled and used in any dish requiring capers.

Viola spp.

pansy, Johnny-jump-up

Annuals, sun or partial shade, regular water

- **CUISINE** Flavors are extremely mild and slightly sweet.
- **COOKING TIPS** These delightful flowers are easy to grow and add a splash of color to salads; also make a good garnish on cakes and other desserts. Many have contrasting petals that look like little faces, making them fun for children and adults alike.

Heirloom vegetables

Heirloom vegetables—old, open-pollinated varieties that have stood the test of time and yielded rich and tasty crops—are living artifacts. They are a reservoir of genetic diversity, and this is reflected in their wonderful shapes, sizes, colors, and flavors.

Before the advent of industrialized agriculture, farmers saved the seeds of their best plants from year to year. The selection criteria included the size of the fruit, the taste, yield, and ease of harvest. They chose those that thrived in their particular soil or climate. So, over the years, they improved the quality of their crops. They traded or sold the seeds to neighboring farmers. The result was a rich heritage of tasty produce that we now call "heirloom."

Modern produce is also bred and selected, but for quite different purposes. The long distances that many vegetables travel from farm to table mean that they must be sturdy enough to survive. Varieties are therefore selected for their tough skins and firm flesh, not inherently bad qualities, but this often means that flavor and color are no longer prime considerations. Commercial vegetables are also typically picked before they are fully ripe to ensure that they are firm enough, but many do not go on to achieve their fullest flavor and color. Standard producers of vegetables also rely on very few varieties because they are mainly interested in crops that are quick growing, disease-free, easily harvested, and economical, giving a reliable, predictable crop in accordance with the supermarkets' specifications. Thus diversity is scarce.

The color of different vegetables is caused by the presence of chemical pigments. The green pigment of vegetables is caused by the presence of chlorophyll, the yellow/orange colors of vegetables are because of the presence of carotenoids, and the red/blue coloring of some vegetables (e.g., blackberries and red cabbage) are caused by anthocyanins.

Growing vegetables

Grow your own vegetables to save money, eat well, and reduce your carbon footprint. By growing heirloom varieties, you not only have the best-quality vegetables but are helping to preserve a valuable heritage.

Finding heirloom seeds

Home gardeners and local farmers have been carrying on the tradition of preserving heirloom vegetable varieties, harvesting the mature fruit and drying the seed for next year. There are seed exchanges and societies dedicated to saving and distributing seed, and a number of good catalog sources. Some nurseries are joining the trend, carrying a variety of heirloom seeds. They provide a wide diversity of flavors and colors for everything from tomatoes to potatoes.

Growing heirlooms

  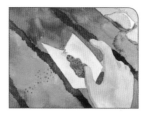  

1 Prepare soil Growing healthy and tasty annual vegetables depends on well-prepared soil. Whether using a gas-powered rototiller or getting exercise by double digging the beds, having good tilth is important to these short-lived plants. Dig the soil well, fork in plenty of compost, and rake out large stones or clods.

2 Add soil nutrients To keep the soil friable and nutrient-rich, organic additions (such as well-rotted compost) can't be beat.

3 Sowing the seeds Most vegetables do best when the seed is sown where the plants are to grow, avoiding the need to transplant seedlings. Very fine seed is best mixed in a plastic bag with an equal quantity of horticultural sand before sowing. This mix can then be scattered onto the growing medium using a piece of card folded in two.

4 Thinning and watering With very fine seed, thinning may be necessary after they begin to sprout, but large seed is easy to space at the correct gaps when sowing.

5 Harvesting Most vegetables are annuals, growing and producing a crop in one year. When the biennials, such as onions, leeks, and garlic, are grown from seed, they are ready for harvest in their second year. A few other vegetables, such as artichokes and asparagus, are perennials and can be harvested year after year.

Sowing seeds in pots

Edible plants will grow inside any container, but the container must be deep enough to allow room for the plant's roots to spread out and for there to be sufficient growing medium in the container for the plant to take up enough nutrients.

EQUIPMENT NEEDED

- watering can
- pots
- trowel
- scissors
- wire
- string
- compost
- seed trays
- sieve
- dibber
- labels
- indelible pen
- pencil

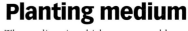

Planting medium

The medium in which your vegetables are grown will determine how well they grow. When using large containers make sure you crock the pot (cover the drainage hole with pebbles or broken shards of pot) to make sure that the holes do not become blocked with compost.

Seed spacing

Sow very fine seed on the surface of the compost and sieve a fine layer of compost over it. Not all seed germinates, so allow for 50 percent more seed than you wish to grow. If you are lucky and all of the seeds grow, you will need to thin the seedlings so that they do not compete for light and grow too spindly.

Planting vegetables

Vegetables can be planted by sowing seeds in trays and transplanting them into containers or the ground once seedlings have developed. They can also be sown directly into seed beds. The method you use will vary from plant to plant, and will depend on growing conditions.

Hardening off

Acclimatize young plants to outdoor conditions by putting them outside during the day and bringing them inside at night when the temperature drops. To produce early crops of plants, they need to be put outside as soon as any frosts are finished. Using a cut-down bottle over a pot is ideal for keeping the plant warm and protecting it from attacks by pests and diseases.

LABELING YOUR SEEDS

It is important to keep track of what has been sown where. Label your seedlings so you do not end up sowing seeds in the same beds twice.

Transplanting seedlings

Seeds are usually sown in seed trays and then transplanted into their containers when they are large enough to handle (once leaves have formed):

1 Using a pencil, remove the seedling from the tray and pick it up gently by the leaves rather than the stem (the stem bruises easily).

2 Make a hole in the new compost with the dibber.

3 Gently drop the seedling into the hole.

4 Firm the compost carefully around the newly planted seedling.

5 Water lightly.

Harvesting times

Different vegetables need harvesting at different times of the year.

• Harvest garlic, spring onions, and shallots in early summer.

• Harvest onions in the fall and leeks from fall onward.

• Carrots should be harvested as they reach the appropriate size. Water the container before harvesting those carrots that have grown to maturity so that you do not disturb the remaining ones.

• Pull beetroot from the ground at different stages of development depending on the size desired. Fork up carefully and twist off the tops (do not cut them or they will bleed). Use the young leaves in salads.

• Radishes will be ready for harvesting within 4 to 8 weeks of sowing, depending on the variety.

• About 3 months after planting, potatoes should be fully formed and flowering. Store any potatoes that you do not want to use immediately in a cool, dark place.

DRYING YOUR OWN SEEDS

Preserve garden diversity by drying your own seeds and encouraging old varieties to thrive and flourish. This a cheaper and more satisfying method of growing your own vegetables, avoiding waste as well as allowing gardeners to share seeds and encourage heirloom species to grow.

Directory

Not all edible plants are hardy, and different kinds of vegetable will need attention in different ways and at different times.

Climbing vegetables

Some plants are ideal for growing vertically because they become unwieldy if left to grow on the ground. Tomatoes and some varieties of cucumber are best grown vertically, and beans grow as both bushes or as vertically climbing plants. Pole beans can climb quite tall, and in some cases may need a large structure to grow on.

Lagenaria siceraria
bottle gourd

Annual climbing vine, sun, regular water
- **CUISINE** The bottle gourd, also known as the calabash, is a vine grown for its fruit that can either be harvested young and used as a vegetable, or be harvested mature, dried, and used as a bottle, utensil, or even pipe—hence the name.
- **GROWING TIPS** The bottle gourd is a running or climbing vine with lush, large leaves that are either light or dark green. The dark green can be a solid color, regular or irregular stripes, or an irregular blotch. The size of the fruit varies from 2–12 inches (5–30 cm) in diameter and from 4–42 inches (10–100 cm) in length. It thrives in a hot to moderately warm, humid climate, and has adapted to a variety of soils (from sandy to moderately heavy) but always needs good drainage.
- **COOKING TIPS** The bottle gourd is frequently used in southern Chinese cuisine in either stir-fries or soups. The Chinese name for calabash is hulu or huzi in Mandarin, and in Japan, where it is known as kanpyo, it is sold in the form of dried, marinated strips, which are used in place of seafood in vegetarian sushi. The shoots, tendrils, and leaves may also be eaten as greens. The delicate, nutty flavor adds greatly to hot curries and cooling yogurt dishes, such as raita. It can be used like squash but has a firmer, crisper texture.

Phaseolus coccineus

French bean

Perennial, full sun, regular water

- **VARIETIES** French beans are generally easier to grow than runners. There are two types of French beans: dwarf varieties and climbers.
- **GROWING TIPS** Choose a well-drained, sunny spot. Make sure it's sheltered, as French beans can be vulnerable to chilly winds. Young French bean pods are far tastier than mature pods, which are stringy and dull in flavor. The pods you pick should be smooth in appearance and ought to snap easily when you bend them. If you can see bean-shapes bulging along the pods, they are past their best. Frequent picking accelerates the plant's natural tendency to produce pods over a long period.

Phaseolus lunatus

lima bean

Annual, sun, regular water

- **GROWING TIPS** Lima beans can be harvested fresh or dried.
- **VARIETIES** Many of the heirloom varieties have interesting and beautiful variegation. The 'Dixie Speckled Butterpea' is red-speckled and the 'Christmas-pole Lima' has very large white beans with dark red splashes.
- **COOKING TIPS** Limas may be easier to shell if you use scissors to cut the pods open. Do not eat raw; they contain a cyanide compound that is deactivated only by cooking.

Phaseolus vulgaris

pole/runner bean

Annual, sun, regular water

- **GROWING TIPS** Beans are either harvested young for their tender pods and young seeds, or when the pods and seeds have dried. Plant beans 1 inch deep, every 3 inches, in rich soil when it has warmed up. Space the rows about 2½ feet apart in a sunny location. Bush types require no support but the climbing, vining type will need a netted climbing frame or wigwam installed before planting.
- **VARIETIES** There are countless varieties. Two long-time favorite green pole beans are 'Kentucky Wonder' and 'Blue Lake'.
- **COOKING TIPS** Pick when the beans are plump, shell, and use in soups or cook until tender as a side dish. Do not eat raw; they may cause severe intestinal problems.

Pisum sativum

pea

Annual, full sun, regular water

- **VARIETIES** Peas are nearly impossible to find in many markets, but they are very undemanding in the garden. They are one of the oldest known food crops, having been cultivated since about 7,000 B.C. Heirloom varieties, such as 'Lincoln' and 'Little Marvel' were introduced around 1908 and remain standards in the garden. Edible pod peas, including sugar snap and snow peas (also known as mangetout or *pois gourmand*) are relative newcomers to commerce, but have been grown for 300 years or more.
- **GROWING TIPS** All are at their very best when grown at home for immediate consumption. As they require cool temperatures, they are a good early spring (or winter, in very mild climate zones) crop.

Psophocarpus tetragonolobus

winged bean

Annual, full sun, regular water

- **CUISINE** Every part of this plant is edible, from the nutty roots to the leaves that can be cooked like spinach, to the nutritious bean pods with their winged edges. Two selections of this unusual bean mean that almost all climate zones can grow it. The one called 'Thai Winged Bean' is suitable for warm zones, while the 'Hunan Winged Bean' will thrive in more northerly zones. Grow like peas. The vines climb by tendrils and need a support. Harvest the pods when they are plump.

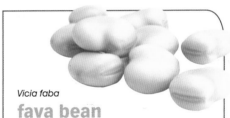

Vicia faba

fava bean

Annual, sun, regular water

- **GROWING TIPS** This Mediterranean native is rarely offered in markets, so growing your own is an obvious way to ensure its availability. Also known as the broad bean, it has been cultivated worldwide for so long that no one is sure where it originated.
- **COOKING TIPS** The pods are thick and fuzzy and must be discarded, and the thin shell of each bean must also be removed. One of the simplest ways to prepare and eat the beans is to drop them into salted, boiling water and drain after one minute. When cool, pinch off a bit of the skin and squeeze out the bean. Eat immediately or use in any number of soups or salads, or purée as a hummus-like dip.

Vigna umbellate

red rice bean

Annual, full sun, regular water

- **VARIETIES** There are many different species of beans that are unique to Asian cuisine and this is one of them. The red rice bean produces tiny red beans slightly larger than a grain of rice. They are often added to rice dishes for flavor, texture, and protein. As easy to grow as any climbing bean, they make a tasty, interesting addition to the gourmet garden. The hairy annual vine bears yellow flowers—the beans can also be yellow.
- **CUISINE** A typical dish of Louisiana Creole cuisine, red beans and rice is traditionally made on Mondays (wash day.) It consists of red beans, vegetables (onion and celery), spices (thyme, cayenne pepper, and bay leaf), and pork bones left over from Sunday's dinner (traditionally ham). These ingredients are cooked together slowly in a pot, simmering away over a low heat while clothes are scrubbed. It is served on rice and has become a Monday lunch special in restaurants in Louisiana.

Vigna unguiculata

long bean

Annual, full sun, regular water

- **VARIETIES** One variety is known as the 'Yard Long Bean', and its incredible beans actually grow over 3 feet (90 cm) long. Other varieties mature at 1–2 feet (30–60 cm) in length. There are also selections that have strikingly colored beans from pink to brilliant red.
- **CUISINE** All have a mild flavor and no strings, and can be served like other snap beans. They grow by twining up poles and need support.

Vigna unguiculata

black-eyed pea

Annual, full sun, regular water

- **VARIETIES** There are many names and varieties of this bean, including southern pea, cow pea, and field pea.
- **CUISINE** Many traditional southern U.S. dishes employ nutty-tasting black-eyed peas, which are a typical food at New Year, to ensure 12 months of good luck. The species also includes other varieties, such as the long beans of Asia. All originated in Africa, with the black-eyed pea being spread abroad by émigrés and slaves.
- **GROWING TIPS** Grow with support for the twining vines. The beans are harvested when young, with the seeds fully developed, or dried for storage.

Zea mays

corn

Annual, full sun, regular water

- **VARIETIES** Corn varieties have been selected and saved for thousands of years by Native American peoples, so it is no wonder that there are a multitude of these old selections still in cultivation. The heirloom varieties of this wind-pollinated plant will come true from seed only when they are grown isolated from each other.

  These original varieties were grown mainly for their dried, mature kernels, and were either selected for their popping ability or for milling into flour. Many bear names that attest to their early Indian growers. 'Hopi Blue' is a blue dent corn good for making the recently popularized blue corn tortillas, 'Cherokee Long Ear' has kernels in red, blue, orange, white, and yellow, making it a decorative corn that's also useful for popping, and 'Black Aztec' may have actually originated with the Iroquois nation. Later agriculturists began selecting varieties for their sweetness as a fresh vegetable. Among the many sweet corn varieties available are 'Stowell's Evergreen White' (developed in 1848), 'Country Gentleman' (1890), a shoe-peg type whose kernels grow randomly instead of in rows, and the standard 'Golden Bantam' (c.1900).

- **GROWING TIPS** Corn should be planted in full sun, long after the risk of any frost has passed. Different varieties of corn should be separated so that they do not cross pollinate. Plant in well-draining soil with a temperature of around 60°F (16°C) for the seeds to germinate.

Root and tuberous vegetables

These are actually plant roots that are used as vegetables. They are generally storage organs, which are enlarged to store energy in the form of carbohydrates. Those with a high carbohydrate concentration (in the form of starch) are important staple foods because they are cheap and easy to grow, and filling to eat.

Apium graveolens var. rapaceum

celeriac

Biennial grown as annual, full sun, regular water

- **CUISINE** Grown for its root instead of its stalks or leaves, celeriac (also known as celery root) is native to the Mediterranean, where it is still grown and enjoyed in a number of ways. Its flavor is intense (a mixture of celery and parsley), and its sturdy texture (if not overcooked) makes it useful in various ways, from adding flavor and texture in salads to accompanying roasted meats. In France celery root in a remoulade sauce is an old favorite. Celeriac and potatoes can also be combined in a classic Scandinavian dish by being cooked together and puréed. Celeriac also combines well with leeks and avgolemono sauce in a traditional Greek dish.

Beta vulgaris

beet

Annual, sun, regular water

- **GROWING TIPS** This root vegetable is easy to grow, and at its sweet and tender best when pulled fresh from the earth and cooked within hours.
- **VARIETIES** The standard variety is deep red and bleeds into anything it's cooked with. 'Chioggia' (Italian, pre-1840), on the other hand, is almost white and has concentric rings, alternating red and pale pink. Although these colors fade somewhat when cooked, the roots are mildly sweet and tasty.
- **COOKING TIPS** Cook beets whole with their skin on and peel when tender.

Brassica rapa

turnip

Annual, full sun, regular water

- **CUISINE** They are crisp fleshed and somewhat spicy, like their radish relatives. In France they are glazed with sugar and butter, and served with thickly sliced ham; in India and Pakistan they may be curried with meat and spices to make *shabdeg*.
  - **VARIETIES** Those varieties that have survived the test of time tend to be mild and sweet, or chosen for their keeping qualities. 'White Egg' is one of the oldest in the United States (pre-1880s), although the 'Purple Top Milan' from Italy and 'Navet des Vertus Marteau' from France probably pre-date it.
  - **GROWING TIPS** Being biennials, several plants should be left to flower in the second year if saving seed.

Daucus carota

carrot

Annual, sun, regular water

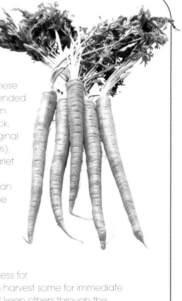

- **VARIETIES** Astonishingly, the familiar orange carrot only appeared on the scene in the 1700s. Its white and purple relatives originated hundreds of years earlier. Descendants of these earliest selections are available as 'Lunar White' (possibly descended from the Middle Ages), and the much later introduction 'Belgian White' (early 1800s). Purple carrots are now making a comeback, but they were around in the early 1300s in Italy. Some of the original orange varieties are still widely grown: 'Danvers Half Long' (1870s), 'Rouge Demi-Longue de Chantenay' (1830s), and 'Nantes Scarlet Half Long' (pre-1900).
- **GROWING TIPS** Be sure to prepare the soil to a depth greater than the expected length of the carrot variety, because they become misshapen and stunted if they encounter anything but fine tilth. Properly stored, carrots can retain their crunch and sweetness for months, so harvest some for immediate eating, but keep others through the winter for a tasty and nutritious winter vegetable.

Ipomoea batatas

sweet potato

Perennial grown as an annual

- **GROWING TIPS** Sweet potatoes are easy to grow, but they do need a few things to grow really well such as carefully dug, compost-rich soil. They also need drainage. Plant them in raised beds or on mounds 6 inches high. This will avoid tubers rotting in wet weather. Sweet potatoes crop best at temperatures between 70 and 80°F (21–26°C). Keep them well watered, feeding every other week with a high-potassium liquid feed.
- **VARIETIES** There are around 400 different varieties of sweet potato.
- **COOKING TIPS** Sweet potatoes can be baked, boiled, fried, broiled, or frozen. Before cooking, scrub the skin and trim off any bruised or woody portions. A freshly baked or boiled sweet potato is delicious and nutritious. You need only to add a pat of butter or serve it plain. It can also be added to soups and stews, and it is a perfect first food for babies, because of its naturally sweet taste.

Pastinaca sativa

parsnip

Annual, full sun, regular water

- **VARIETIES** This sweet root vegetable was from the beginning such a winner that little improvement by selection has been needed. One of the older varieties is 'Hollow Crown', which was already popular in the 1820s.
- **GROWING TIPS** The long roots need loose soil that is very well prepared to the depth you wish the roots to reach, i.e., at least 12 inches (30 cm).

Raphanus sativa

radish

Annual, full sun, regular water

- **VARIETIES** Here's another root vegetable that has spanned the globe in its history of culinary cultivation. Probably native to the eastern Mediterranean, it went in all directions and shows all the variations inherent in its evolutionary history. Black radishes, such as the 'Round' and 'Long Black Spanish' varieties, have been grown for centuries in Europe. They are favorites in cold climates, where their very spicy flavor can be preserved all winter. They are much drier than some of the other, quite succulent varieties, but can be eaten raw or cooked. Daikon-type radishes are popular in Asian cuisines from Japan to India, and everywhere in between. Some have long, carrot-shaped roots, whereas others are globes. Most have white flesh, with some in green and red. In the West they have descriptive names like 'Chinese White Winter' and 'Japanese Minowase Daikon'. Smaller, crispy and piquant varieties, such as 'French Breakfast' and 'Sparker White Tip' (also known as 'Scarlet Turnip White Tip'), are popular as additions to salads and when served as crudités with salt and butter (in France) or a dipping sauce (America).
- **GROWING TIPS** Radishes are very easy to grow in summer and winter. They will grow very quickly and will need thinning as the seedlings develop. Summer harvested radishes are small and mature fast. Winter radishes are larger. Radishes can be planted in containers of most sizes as well as directly in the ground. Because they grow quickly, it is sometimes a good idea to plant them in a shared container alongside vegetables that will mature later, such as beans.

Solanum tuberosum

potato

Grown as annual, full sun, water regularly

- **VARIETIES** Originating in the Andes, the potato has won the hearts of cooks worldwide. The edible tubers are offshoots of the underground stem and come in shades of white to buff and yellow, or red and even purple. There are two main types of potato, those with dry flesh (great for baking) and those with waxy flesh, whose starch adds the best texture to soups and stews. Grow one of the original Peruvian purple varieties or try any of the heirloom selections that have spread elsewhere.
- **GROWING TIPS** Potatoes require well-drained, sandy loam to produce smooth and shapely tubers. Plant them from 2-inch (5-cm) long tubers with at least two "eyes." If your soil is less than perfect, you can plant the tubers only 2 inches (5 cm) deep, pull more soil up around them as the shoots appear, mulching over them as they grow. The tubers will form in the mulch layer and are easy to harvest. Pick new potatoes when the plants begin to flower, and mature ones when the plant dies down.

Tragopogon porrifolius

salsify

Annual, full sun, regular water

- **VARIETIES** There are actually two distinct plants called salsify, with this one being perhaps the most commonly available for the gourmet garden. It is also variously known as white salsify or oyster plant.
- **CUISINE** The carrot-like root adds a mild flavor as a foil for other ingredients, although it may be mashed, glazed, or creamed, again like a carrot.
- **GROWING TIPS** Sow in spring as soon as the frosts have finished. Salsify takes nearly four months from planting to harvest. Pull out the scraggly roots, scrub well, and peel before cooking. The flesh may stain the skin and will discolor immediately, so immerse it in acidulated water until ready to cook. Use lemon juice to remove stains on hands.

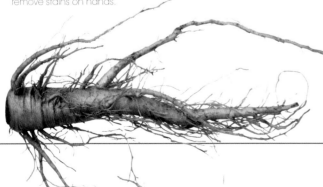

Squash vegetables

Squash vegetables belong to the gourd family, along with zucchini, marrows, and pumpkins. They are fleshy vegetables that can be grown outdoors. The distinctions between the different types are blurred, and they grow in various shapes.

Squashes have recently become more popular in gourmet cuisine, replacing more traditional ingredients like zucchini and pumpkin in dishes such as curries. Despite their growing popularity in cuisine, they continue to compete with the zucchini because, unlike the other members of the gourd family, it does not need to be peeled or de-seeded.

There are summer and winter squash varieties, summer squashes being nonstandard-shaped marrows with soft skins and pale, soft flesh. They are bland in flavor, whereas the winter squashes, such as the Table Ace, Hubbard Squash, Butternut, Crown Prince, and Sweet Dumpling, have firm, orange, fibrous flesh and are well worth the effort of growing in warmer climates.

Vegetable spaghetti is a winter squash and an excellent novelty. Once boiled and sliced in half, the seeds are removed and the spaghetti-like strands can be scraped out with a fork, giving homegrown spaghetti.

Cucumis anguria
gherkin

Annual, full sun, regular water

- **CUISINE** This cucumber relative, which originated in India, is known for the distinctive gherkin pickle, but it can also be eaten raw like any cucumber.
- **GROWING TIPS** It is best suited to warmer climates, where it grows as a vigorous vine. Each plant will yield hundreds of small fruits.

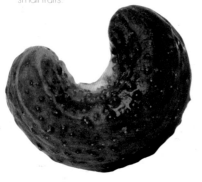

Cucumis metuliferus
African horned cucumber

Annual, full sun, regular water

- **CUISINE** This unusual "fruit" is related to cucumbers, but its sweet-sour flavor is more suited to desserts than salads. It may be known by the African name *kiwano*, or jelly melon. When ripe, it has an orange skin that encloses a lime green, jelly-like pulp. Eat as is or squeeze for a truly exotic juice. It is easy to grow wherever melons are grown.
- **GROWING TIPS** Seeds must be barely covered when sowing, and may profit from being started indoors.

Cucumis sativus
cucumber

Annual, full sun, regular water

- **VARIETIES** This vegetable has been carried around the world, and each nation has had an effect on its evolution. There are some broad categories that can be applied to cucumbers according to their origins and uses. The American pickling "cukes" are usually relatively short and warty with thinner skins than the American slicing "cukes" with their smooth, dark green skin (which also have the least flavor). One of the best heirloom American varieties is 'Lemon Cuke', which is round and the color of a lemon. Introduced in 1894 to the United States from its native Australia, it has a mild flavor. Middle Eastern cucumbers were developed in Israel in the early 1900s, and are slim, smooth skinned, and tasty. Asian cucumbers have the deepest flavor and best crunch. Their English language names, such as 'Chinese Yellow', 'Thai Green', and 'Hmong Red', indicate their place of origin.

Curcubita pepo

marrow

Annual
- **VARIETIES** Until recently, the marrow—large, oblong, and striped—was the dominant member of the gourd section of the cucumber family. There are several varieties including the 'Green Bush', 'Early Gem', 'Long Green Trailing', and 'Long White Trailing'.
- **COOKING TIPS** Marrows are used widely as a boiled vegetable or an edible casing for a more exciting stuffing.
- **GROWING TIPS** Marrows can be grown as a trailing variety or as a bush where space is scarce. A sunny spot, protected from strong winds, is essential.

Cucurbita pepo, C. maxima, C. mixta, C. moschata

squash and pumpkin

Annual, full sun, regular water
- **VARIETIES** Related to cucumbers and melons, the group includes summer squashes (thin-skinned), winter squashes (thick-skinned, keeps well), and pumpkins (also thick-skinned, with the deepest flavor). The line between winter squash and pumpkin tends to blur. Many varieties that originated from the species *Cucurbita pepo* have the same dense texture as pumpkins. There are dozens of old favorites that can be served as a savory vegetable or creamed into sweet pies or cakes.

Luffa acutanbula

angled loofah

Annual, full sun, regular water
- **CUISINE** This narrow, squash-like vegetable is as mild in flavor and as versatile as summer squash. Being very perishable, it is seldom available in markets or is of inferior quality by the time it is sold.
- **GROWING TIPS** Grow it just as you would any other squash. Its next of kin, the sponge gourd (*L. aegyptiaca*), is grown for its fibrous interior that, when dried, can be used as a washing cloth.

Momordica charantia

bitter gourd

Climbing annual, full sun, regular water
- **CUISINE** From Southeast Asia, it's also known as bitter cucumber, balsam pear, karela, and ampalaya. Bitter gourd is an acquired taste, and is grown mainly for the immature fruits, although the young leaves and tips are also edible.
- **GROWING TIPS** The seed has a hard skin and needs warm, moist soil conditions in order to germinate. Bitter gourd is a long-season, high-humidity, and warm-climate vine plant and needs supporting.
- **COOKING TIPS** The bitter gourd is actually a member of the squash family, resembling a cucumber with bumpy skin. It lends itself well to stuffing and can also be steamed or used in stir-fries and soups Garlic and chili peppers are often added to to offset the bitter taste.

Stem and bulb vegetables

The main edible part of these vegetables is their bulb, the underground enlarged structure just above the roots where the plant's nutrient reserves are stored. Bulbs are higher in carbohydrates and lower in water content than stems, flowers, or leafy vegetables.

Allium fistulosum

scallion / spring onion

Annual, full sun, regular water

- **VARIETIES** Scallions are known under many names, including spring onions, green onions, bunching onions, and Welsh onions. Grow scallions in your garden or even along the edge of your flower beds— their bright green color and tall leaves look striking.
- **GROWING TIPS** The scallion produces the highest yields and best quality in late spring. However, day length does not affect production so, unlike bulb onions, scallions are produced throughout the year. Plant scallions ½ inch (1.5 cm) deep in single rows 6 to 8 inches (15 to 20 cm) apart. Plants should be ½ to 1 inch (1.5 to 2.5 cm) apart. Scallions mature in 8 to 10 weeks in summer and 12 to 14 weeks in winter. Cut off any flower stems that appear—you want all the plant's energy going into swelling the bulb and not setting seed. Stop watering once the onions have swollen and begin to ripen. Harvest the plants when they look big enough to eat, or are about 12 to 14 inches (30 to 40 cm) high. Do not cut the roots or leaves.
- **CUISINE** Recipes will call for using either just the white part, or both the white and green part of the scallion. Generally, the white part is cooked, and the green part is used as a garnish or in salad preparations. In a pinch you can substitute the green part for chives.

Allium spp.

shallots

Grown as annuals, full sun, regular water

- **CUISINE** Shallots are probably the extreme result of the kind of selection that is embodied in the heirloom varieties. They originate from the same species as the regular culinary onion, and are prized for their very mild taste.
- **VARIETIES** Believed to have originated in western Asia, shallots were brought to Britain by returning Crusaders. For many years the shallot was considered a distinct species, but it has now been classified as a member of the ageratum or lily group within *Allium cepa*. The main characteristic of this group is the multiplication of bulbs through lateral cloves, more like garlic than onions. Different varieties are chosen by gardeners for their flavor, shape, and resistance to disease.

Allium spp.
leeks

Grown as annuals, full sun, regular water

- **CUISINE** Leeks are a type of *Allium* that never forms a bulb, with the tightly furled leaves forming a tasty vertical cylinder of growth. Either sow seed or buy seedlings for an early start (they take an average of 130 days to maturity). The flavor is immediately developed with the briefest of cooking, and the silken texture adds to soups or stands alone as a side dish.
- **GROWING TIPS** Sow seeds in spring and transplant the seedlings once they are 6 inches (15 cm) tall. Make a narrow hole using a dibber and drop the seedling in it. To increase the length of the white shank, keep earthing up the plants. Space them 4 inches (10 cm) apart for smaller leeks, and 6 inches (15 cm) for bigger ones.
- **COOKING TIPS** The white part is the most popular, but the green part adds flavor to puréed soups and stews; it is often combined with potatoes in a cold soup called *vichyssoise*.

Allium spp.
garlic

Grown as annuals, full sun, regular water

- **CUISINE** Garlic is grown by separating and planting the individual cloves. It has few leaves, and the bases swell into the succulent and flavorful cloves whose complex flavor is essential in many cuisines. Different varieties extend the season and provide subtle differences of flavor.
- **VARIETIES** 'Christo' produces a good yield, and 'Russian Red' is hardy, with a good flavor.
- **GROWING TIPS** To grow garlic, plant cloves in late autumn with the tips just below the surface of the soil, spacing them approximately 4 inches (10 cm) apart.

Allium spp.
onions

Grown as annuals, full sun, regular water

- **CUISINE** Onions and their relatives owe their underground goodness to a compact array of leaves that arise from a root system below the surface of the soil. This is very different from many other root vegetables whose goodness comes from an enlarged underground stem storing tasty sugars and starches. Everyone is familiar with the widely sold bulbous onions whose many succulent layers (i.e., swollen leaf bases) are encased in a few dry, papery ones. If not harvested, they endure a dormant winter season before converting the stored carbohydrates into a flower stalk.
- **VARIETIES** Green and bunching onions are juvenile forms of the same varieties as those grown to full size. The former have not had time to begin making a thickened bulb, whereas the latter are a little more mature but are still harvested for their sweet, small, bulbous bottoms as well as their tasty green tops. Planted thickly and left to mature, these varieties also produce the smaller dry onions known variously as baby, boiler, creamer, pearl, or pickler onions. Some of the tastiest of the mature onions have less of the sulfurous compounds that lead to tears and a hotter flavor. Old favorites include the cipollini types from Italy, but onions have been developed everywhere from Australia to the United States.

  The mildest onions have a moderate amount of sugar, which can be mitigated by the action of a complex chemical reaction that starts as soon as the onion is cut. A normally benign chemical is then brought into contact with an enzyme that creates the tear-producing (and aromatic) quality for which they are famous.
- **GROWING TIPS** Growing conditions can also influence taste, so limit the amount of sulfur in the soil, and water regularly for a less concentrated flavor, letting the inherent sweetness shine through. Onion, shallots, and leeks can be grown from seed, which is very fine. The best results may be had by sowing in seed flats or small containers before teasing the seedlings apart for planting out. Many varieties may also be available as small bulbs, called "sets," that will mature earlier than the seed-grown kind.

Allium tuberosum

Chinese chives

Perennial, full sun, regular water

- **CUISINE** Also known as garlic chives, the plant is grown for its leaves, which have a mild garlic flavor. The leaves can be snipped with scissors and added to salads, soups, and any other dish that involves ordinary chives. They are added to stir-fried dishes and folded into spring rolls.
- **GROWING TIPS** Since garlic chives grow from small bulbs, it is easiest to buy and plant a potted clump, but they can also be sown from seed..

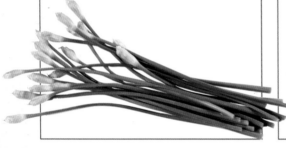

Apium graveolens

celery

Biennial, sun, regular water

- **GROWING TIPS** Growing celery is a challenge. It thrives where growing seasons are long, moist, and cool—though most varieties won't tolerate frost. The celery plant is slender and stands about 2 to 3 feet (60 to 90 cm) tall. It has 3 to 5 segmented leaves, and flowers with small white petals. Buy started celery plants at a nursery. Otherwise, start seeds indoors about 8 weeks before the last expected frost. Harden off seedlings, then transplant them to the garden when temperatures are reliably above 50°F (10°C). Set plants slightly deeper than they were growing in their flats, spacing them 6 to 10 inches (15 to 25 cm) apart. Mulch to retain moisture and deter weeds.
  The celery you buy in the store has been artificially "blanched" by depriving it of light. This gives the stalks a more subtle flavor. Your homegrown celery will have a darker, deeper green color. You can blanch your celery to prevent it from being too bitter by covering the plants to protect them from the sun. As the plants grow, pile soil up around them to blanch the stems. Having the plants fairly close together will also help blanching. Harvest celery as soon as it's large enough to use. Either cut off individual stems as they develop color, or pull the entire plant and cut off the roots.
- **CUISINE** Celery is well known as a classic salad ingredient, best enjoyed raw, while fresh and crispy and full of flavor. By slowly frying to soften with carrot and onion, celery can also add flavor to a soup or stew. Of course, celery is also commonly known as one of the important components of a Bloody Mary cocktail.

Asparagus officinalis

asparagus

Full sun, water regularly

- **CUISINE** Nothing beats homegrown asparagus for the best flavor and texture. The crisp spears are sweet and nutty when raw, and deeply satisfying when steamed or quickly sautéed. Grilling on the barbecue or roasting in the oven also brings out an additional dimension to their flavor.
- **VARIETIES** 'Precoce d'Argenteuil' is a traditional Italian variety excellent for blanching to produce pure white spears. This is done by excluding all the light from the growing shoots. When treated this way, asparagus spears must be immediately chilled and kept cold until cooking. Growing your own makes the journey from harvest to kitchen the best possible solution to this dilemma. Other old varieties include some with purple coloration, such as 'Violetta de Albinga'.
- **GROWING TIPS** Asparagus needs very rich soil. It can be grown from seed or roots. From seed to first harvest will take 4 years, whereas the roots are from plants already 2 or more years old. For those first years, do not harvest the stems. Allow them to mature and feed the enlarging root system. Once they are well established, asparagus spears can be cut to just below soil level for about 6 weeks in spring before they become too slender and tough. These last stems are left to mature, becoming deciduous in fall.

Cynara scolymus

globe artichoke

Perennial, full to part sun,
regular water

- **CUISINE** If ever there was a
  vegetable that children would
  abhor, this is it. Artichokes can be
  rather daunting with their semi-starchy texture
  and the complicated process of eating them,
  which involves scraping off the thin layer of
  concentrated flavor from the lower part of the "leaves"
  (really flower bracts), then dealing with the inedible "choke" to finally get
  to the perfection of the few bites of the "heart." But the mellow, starchy-
  but-green flavor is incredibly popular, and the best kind are freshly
  harvested from your own garden.
- **VARIETIES** One of the standard American varieties, 'Green Globe', has
  been grown since 1863. Many of the varieties grown in Italy, France,
  and other countries that face the Mediterranean are harvested young.
  There, the succulent flower buds are often eaten whole and have little
  of the troublesome "choke." Try 'Purple Romagna'. Plant from seed or
  young plants. Most will be completely to partially deciduous, becoming
  larger and more productive every year. Once established, each plant
  can produce several edible artichokes each season.

Brassica oleracea

kohlrabi

Annual, full sun, regular water

- **VARIETIES** Another of the
  many vegetables that have
  originated from just this one
  species in the cabbage
  family, kohlrabi is widely
  grown in most temper-
  ate and Mediterranean
  climates. There are a few
  old varieties in Europe and North
  America. 'Purple Vienna' and
  'White Vienna' have been
  cultivated for at least two centuries.
- **CUISINE** Although the entire plant
  is edible, the most
  concentrated flavor is
  in the enlarged stem.
  Peeled, it can be
  eaten fresh or pre-
  pared in a number of
  ways to complement
  its mild flavor.

Fruiting vegetables

These include peppers, tomatoes, chilies, and eggplant. They originate in warm climes but have adapted to survive worldwide. They like full sun and regular watering. In their natural habitats they grow vigorously and fruit copiously, but they do need coaxing into fruiting well in colder climates. Try growing them under a cloche or position them in front of a sunny window.

Capsicum annum and other spp.

pepper

Annual, full sun, regular water

- **CUISINE** Used in nearly every cuisine around the world, there are peppers that, when roasted, are as sweet as any other vegetable and those that can cause burning sensations on contact with skin.
- **VARIETIES** Sweet pimento peppers from Italy, 'Topepo Rosso' and 'Quadrato D'asti Rosso', are thick, fleshy red peppers perfect for eating raw. Peperoncini peppers—thin skinned, small green or yellow varieties, perfect for pickling—are represented by Italian and Greek varieties. Mexico, South America, and the Caribbean all have their heirloom varieties. Most peppers need a long, warm growing season (60–95 days), so starting seeds early indoors is a good strategy for northern climes.

Capsicum annum

chilies

Perennial, full sun, regular water

- **GROWING TIPS** Grown as ornamental decorative plants and for their fruits—these can then be harvested when green, for some cuisines, or be left to ripen to red. Some will turn orange, yellow, or even chocolate brown, depending on the variety. Better results are achieved in higher temperatures and humidity.
- **VARIETIES** You can try growing something as common as the Jalapeño, Anaheim, or Serrano, or experiment with something more exotic like the Thai Dragon Pepper.
- **CUISINE** Chilies are well known for their fiery flavor and are used to spice up soups, stir-fries, and curries. Each variety has a different heat strength, so it is important to know what you are dealing with before adding it to your cooking—sometimes only the tiniest amount is enough to give a real kick to a recipe.

Lycopersicon esculentum

tomato

Annual, full sun, regular water

- **VARIETIES** What is it with the solanum family? Eggplants, peppers, potatoes, and tomatoes have been molded to almost every climate zone in the world, no matter what their original native habitat. Tomatoes, once thought by Europeans to be poisonous (though many members of this family are), have become an essential ingredient in a myriad of culinary traditions. There are now thousands to choose from. Color, juiciness (or its opposite, meatiness), and flavor are all characteristics that have been propagated. There are myriads of the red-skinned, red-fleshed varieties, but how about green, yellow, orange, chocolate, purple, pink, or striped ones to dress up a salad or dinner plate?
- **GROWING TIPS** Outdoor tomatoes are a tender crop, so it is important that you grow them in a sheltered, warm spot against a south-facing wall. During the winter, dig the soil thoroughly and add garden compost. If space is short, outdoor tomatoes can be grown in pots or growing bags placed on the open ground or on balconies or patios. Tomatoes planted in containers will need watering much more frequently and regular feeding will be essential.

Persea americana

avocado

Evergreen tree, full sun, regular water

- **CUISINE** The avocado is the principal ingredient of one of Latin America's best-loved dishes, guacamole. It is easy enough to buy both the ingredient and ready-made guacamole in your local store, but why not try growing this tropical plant in your own garden?
- **GROWING TIPS** The avocado tree is happiest in a tropical environment, though it can tolerate a light frost. While avocados will grow in shade and even between buildings, they are productive only in full sun. They like loose, decomposed granite or sandy loam best, and will not survive in poor drainage.

Physalis philadelphica

tomatillo

Annual, full sun, regular water

- **CUISINE** The tomatillo fruit is surrounded by a paper-like husk formed from the calyx. As the fruit matures, it fills the husk and can split it open by harvest time. The tomatillo has a slightly tart flavor, a bit like a gooseberry, giving an authentic flavor in Mexican green sauces and salsa. Eat raw in dishes such as salsa, but it also tastes good fried in olive oil or when grilled and seasoned with salt and pepper.
- **GROWING TIPS** When growing your own, note that the fruit is ripe when it fills out its papery husk but is still green. If it turns yellow it is still useable, though it will have lost much of its tangy flavor. The plants grow to a height of 3–4 feet (90–120 cm). They are generally available from early spring to fall, and are drought-tolerant. Keep picking the ripe fruit.

Solanum torvum

green pea eggplant

Annual, full sun, regular water

- **CUISINE** This diminutive eggplant is still green when harvested. The pea-sized vegetables are an essential ingredient in authentic Thai dishes, including curries, soups, and stir-fries.
- **GROWING TIPS** They are easy to grow from seed in climates where other eggplants thrive; warmer zones produce larger harvests.

Solanum melongena

eggplant/aubergine

Annual, full sun, regular water

- **VARIETIES** An international traveler, the eggplant has found its way from East Asia to the Middle East, the Mediterranean, and the Americas. The original fruit (actually a berry) was egg shaped, just like hens' eggs. Selection favors a sweeter taste and a greater flesh-to-seed ratio. The colors and sizes seem endless, and run from the purple-streaked light green 'Udmalbet', introduced from a Tamil village in India, to the long, slender purple fruits of 'Ping Tung' from Taiwan. The much larger, slightly lobed 'Rosa Bianca' from Italy is a rose pink; 'Brazilian Oval Orange' ripens from bright orange to nearly red and is delicious grilled or fried; and the fruit of 'Turkish Orange' is very sweet when cooked, as it turns from green to light orange.

Greens & leafy vegetables

This is a huge category of vegetables, ranging from the crisp and sometimes bitter chicory to the sweet-tasting romanesco broccoli.

Most supermarkets carry fewer than six kinds of lettuces, and about the same number of leafy greens, including spinach and kale. Supermarkets have found that it's hard to keep and transport greens, so they now use controlled-atmosphere plastic pillows, and the leaves are exposed to a great number of chemicals. To help you rediscover the wonders and varieties of greens, seed companies have packaged mixes that combine mild-flavored lettuces in a variety of colors, as well as spicier nonlettuce species such as arugula (also known as rocket or roquette), mustard, and leaf radish. But there are dozens of other crops with delicious and distinctive leaves; given how easy they are to grow, why not have a go?

A multitude of green and leafy vegetables can fill up your vegetable plot and provide ample produce for the keen cook. There is nothing like cutting off a few of the best leaves from your garden or patch of greens just minutes before you eat them.

Grow some mild mache (also known as corn salad or lamb's lettuce), salad burnet with its cucumber-like flavor, or peppery watercress. Try Japanese mizuna, Chinese tatsoi, and Thai mustard greens. Young baby spinach and chard are also tasty additions to salads, as are seedlings of beet and carrot.

Growing greens

These kinds of vegetables are often the first port of call for the first-time home gardener. They are thought of as being a good place to start, as they are fairly straightforward to grow and can stock your kitchen with an abundance of tasty vegetables for all seasons.

Sowing seeds

The seeds of most of these species are tiny. Sow them in patches or wide rows so that you can repeatedly cut baby greens, or in single rows to grow plants to maturity. Thin the rows several times as the plants grow, using the thinnings in cooking. Mulch between rows as the plants grow, and stagger sowings for longer production. In hot areas, lettuce might bolt (stop producing new leaves and send up a flower stalk), so make successive plantings to extend the season. Greens are easy to grow in containers of almost any size. Use a good commercial potting mix that is high in organic content.

Watering

Water with a fine rose spray until seedlings are established, gradually deepening the watering to encourage good root systems that will resist wilting as the days get warmer. Most greens require consistently moist soil to do well, and regular watering and plenty of moisture-retaining organic material dug into the ground months before will keep them happy.

Harvesting

Harvest a few leaves as they are needed from leafy greens, allowing for a longer harvest season from a single planting. Harvest outer, more mature leaves first, leaving the inner leaves to continue growing.

1 Cut about two-thirds of a young plant with scissors and it will continue to grow new leaves, or harvest the outer leaves of more mature plants, taking a bit at a time.

2 Submerge the leaves in a bowl of cool water for 10–15 minutes. This will allow grit to sink to the bottom, and hydrate the leaves. Salad spinners are the best way to dry tender greens, though blotting carefully on toweling also works.

Cloches

Every gardener has experienced a crop ruined by an unexpected frost. The use of cloches can help to protect your plants from this and can help to extend the natural growing season. A cloche is like a tiny greenhouse that sits on a garden bed. They come in many shapes and sizes, from dome cloches to tunnel cloches covering several plants.

Cloches are made from plastic or glass held together by a system of wire, plastic, or wooden supports. Plastic cloches are the most practical because they do not break easily and should last for many years. In addition, plastic is much lighter than glass, making it easier to move the cloches around. The one advantage of glass is that the temperature within will be slightly warmer than that of a plastic cloche. On bright, sunny days all cloches must be manually ventilated, to prevent heat buildup, and poorly staked-down cloches can become kites during winter windstorms.

Greenhouses

Whereas cold frames and cloches are relatively inexpensive, greenhouses can be a major purchase. Greenhouses may be made of panes of glass or rigid plastic framed in timber, aluminum, or plastic. Another variation is the hoop-style greenhouse. Greenhouses are often heated to further extend the growing season.

The most important leafy vegetable grown under greenhouse conditions is lettuce. Many different types and varieties of lettuce can be grown under greenhouse conditions, including specialty types. Generally, the looseleaf, butterhead, and romaine or cos types are grown in greenhouses rather than the crisp head types. A crop of lettuce can be produced from seed in about 35 to 45 days.

Cooking with greens

Use baby greens in salads, sandwiches, and as garnishes on other vegetables or grilled meat. Crisp lettuce and other mild, leafy greens can be used to wrap spicy Thai or Vietnamese meat dishes, and can be used in other ethnic dishes and shredded for enclosing in spring rolls.

Cook mature leaves by stir-frying, steaming, or adding them to soups and frittatas, or use them to wrap up packages of rice in recipes for cabbage rolls or stuffed grape leaves.

Finally, note that growing baby greens is a great way to get kids interested in eating salads. Their little fingers are perfect for pinching or snipping the small leaves. They will also have fun swishing them around and cleaning them in water, and spinning them dry. Supplying a delicious dip, perhaps guacamole or hummus, is also a great encourager for children, as they seem to enjoy dipping the crisp leaves into a creamy sauce.

Directory

Green leafy vegetables are among the most widely grown group of vegetables, and contain more vitamins and minerals and fewer calories than any other kind of vegetable.

In general, leafy vegetables do not have extensive roots, therefore gardeners need to concern themselves only with the condition of the topsoil. It is vital that the soil be well supplied with organic matter, nutrients, and water. A good tip is to plant 2 or 3 seeds per plant required—these extra seeds are not necessarily wasted, because when the seedlings begin to crowd, they may be thinned and used for salad. Thinning out is important with leafy vegetables, as overcrowding means that plants are competing with each other for water, light, and nutrients, and can cause a poor yield.

Leafy greens grow best in an open, level area where the soil is loose, rich, and well drained. Although leafy crops tolerate shade better than others, at least 6 hours of sunshine daily will help ensure a higher-quality harvest.

In a commercial setting leafy vegetables are harvested as a whole plant. However, it is best for the home gardener to harvest leaf by leaf. This means that the plant is left in the garden to regenerate more leaves for future harvests. Harvest outer, more mature leaves first, leaving the young, inner leaves to continue growing. Most leafy vegetables will keep up to 2 weeks if stored under cold, moist conditions. Place produce in perforated plastic bags and store in the refrigerator.

The two general uses for green leafy vegetables are as salad crops, which are eaten fresh, and as greens or pot herbs, which are usually cooked before eating. Some green leafy vegetables, including spinach, chard, and endive, can be used either fresh or cooked; hence, they are very versatile for the home garden.

Basella alba

malabar spinach

Perennial, full sun, regular water

- **CUISINE** Malabar spinach is a fast-growing, soft-stemmed vine, reaching about 33 feet (10 m) in length. Its thick, semi-succulent, heart-shaped leaves have a mild flavor, and the stalk is often purple.
- **GROWING TIPS** This spinach substitute is a tropical vine and will not survive the frost. The succulent leaves can be picked at any time once the plants are established. It will grow about 8 to 10 feet (2.5 to 3 m) tall and wide, and produces white-tinged pink flowers. Malabar spinach prefers a humus-rich, sandy loam in full sun.
- **COOKING TIPS** The succulent leaves and stem tips are rich in vitamins A and C and are a good source of iron and calcium. They may be eaten raw in salads, boiled, steamed, stir-fried, or added to soups, stews, tofu dishes, and curries. Or you can use them as a filling for quiche, omelets, savory turnovers, and pies.

Beta vulgaris

chard

Biennial grown as annual, full sun, regular water

- **CUISINE** Often called Swiss chard, this variety of beet is grown for its mild leaves that are packed with vitamins instead of its roots.
- **GROWING TIPS** Sow the seed from spring into early summer, and begin harvesting the outer leaves and stems after about 60 days. In mild winter areas chard can also be sown in fall for a winter to spring harvest. There is a popular strain with colorful stems in yellow, orange, and pink called 'Bright Lights'.
- **COOKING TIPS** Cook the stems separately because they require a longer cooking time.

Brassica oleracea

cabbage

Annual, sun, regular water

- **CUISINE** Early cabbages were loose rosettes of crinkled leaves but, over time, growers selected some that formed tight heads. All the following have much more flavor and interest than the commercially available kind. One of the early loose-leaf varieties is 'Nero di Toscana' (sometimes also called 'Black Palm Tree') that has nearly black, purple leaves. Many heading types are still preserved, including 'Cuor di Bue' (popular 150 years ago), 'Early Jersey Wakefield' (from the 1700s in England), 'Premium Late Flat Dutch' (pre-1840), and 'Perfection Drumhead Savoy' (a Parisian favorite pre-1888).
- **GROWING TIPS** Get an early crop started by setting out seedlings 2 to 3 weeks before the last expected frost. Space seedlings about 2 to 3 feet (60 to 90 cm) apart. A second crop can be planted in midsummer. Even watering is the key to preventing cabbages from splitting.
- **COOKING TIPS** Cabbage is great as a salad vegetable and when added to soups. Methods of preservation, such as pickling and salting, to produce sauerkraut or kimchee, have been perfected in many cuisines.

Brassica oleracea

broccoli (purple sprouting)

Biennial, sun, water moderately

- **CUISINE** Purple-sprouting broccoli is nutritious, easy to cook, and one of the few vegetables that crops well and successively, although it can take up to a year to mature. This striking vegetable has a much more delicate flavor than standard broccoli.
- **GROWING TIPS** An open, sunny site is suitable, but it should not be exposed to buffeting winds. Sow very thinly ½ inch deep in rows that are 6 inches (15 cm) apart. Cover with soil. Thin the seedlings to prevent them from becoming weak and spindly. They should be about 3 inches (7.5 cm) apart in the rows. The seedlings are ready for transplanting when they are 3 inches (7.5 cm) high. Plant firmly, setting the seedlings about 1 inch deeper than they were growing in the seed bed. Water after planting. The time to cut is when the flower shoots ("spears") are well formed, but before the small slower buds have opened. Once in flower the spears are woody and tasteless. The spears are generally 4 to 6 inches long and cropping should continue for about 6 weeks. If you let any of them flower, production will stop at an earlier stage. Traditionally, seed for early spring crops is sown at the beginning of summer, with seedlings transplanted to their final positions at the end of that month. To gain crops in early fall, sow seed of early-cropping types, such as 'Rudolf', in early spring, and plant out in early summer.
- **COOKING TIPS** The leaves, heads, and stalks are all edible, but you may want to trim the stalk to avoid toughness. As they are normally slender and do not need a great deal of cooking, the spears of purple-sprouting broccoli are ideal for stir-fries. They can also be lightly boiled or steamed.

Brassica oleracea

calabrese

Biennial grown as annual, full sun, or partial shade, regular water

- **CUISINE** Italy is the center of broccoli evolution, with many of the heirloom varieties originating there. 'Calabrese Green Sprouting' makes a tasty central head followed by many smaller, tender side shoots. Another Italian with a similar habit is 'De Cicco'. Every part of this plant is edible, including the leaves. 'Romanesco' broccoli produces pale green heads of florets arranged in ornate spirals (broccoli crowns are the immature inflorescences), which in the U.S. may be marketed as 'Broccoflower'.
- **GROWING TIPS** Calabrese, or green sprouting broccoli, can be harvested the same year as planting. From a spring sowing, it is ready for picking by fall. Sow small amounts of calabrese seed at regular intervals to avoid gluts; 2 or 3 seeds should be sown at each spot about 6 inches (15 cm) apart. This avoids having to move seedlings—calabrese does best if it is not moved around. Rows should be 12 inches (30 cm) apart, sow seed 1/2 inch (1 cm) deep. For best results, harvest before the flowers open. Pick Calabrese regularly to ensure the heads are at their tastiest and to encourage the formation of sideshoots. Snap or cut off the heads at the top of the stalk.
- **COOKING TIPS** All are wholesome additions to salads when raw or steamed, sautéed, or baked in casseroles. They will store in the fridge for about a week, but they are definitely at their best when harvested and eaten on the same day.

Brassica oleracea

Brussels sprouts

Annual, sun, regular water

- **CUISINE** Commercially available Brussels sprouts are often harvested after they have become tough and bitter, so growing them at home is a must if you want the sweetest and most tender kind.
- **GROWING TIPS** The small, cabbage-like heads are produced on a tall stalk and may be picked successively as they mature. The lowermost leaves should be removed when the sprouts are harvested. Harvest sprouts before the leaves yellow.
- **COOKING TIPS** Steam briefly and enjoy with a slightly acidic sauce or just a squeeze of citrus. Also good lightly fried with pancetta and walnuts.

Brassica juncea

mustard greens

Annual, sun or midday shade, regular water

- **CUISINE** This genus encompasses a huge variety of plant types, from turnips to bok choy (or pak-choi) cabbages to a wide variety of leafy greens.
- **GROWING TIPS** Leafy types are cool-season annuals that can be sown outdoors after the last frost. Sow again in fall, or grow in cold frames or cool greenhouses over winter. They will become bitter with age, and are best harvested when young. Many will regrow when cut, so snip off young leaves with scissors.
- **COOKING TIPS** Best enjoyed lightly steamed or boiled as a side dish, or added to a stir-fry.

Brassica oleracea var. acephala

kale

Biennial grown as annual, full sun, or partial shade, regular water

- **CUISINE** Kale and related collards are merely leafy cabbages, and their leaves are rich in vitamins A and C. Kale varieties abound from smooth-leafed ones to extremely curled and crimped ones. Collards are another type of kale that do not form a head.
- **GROWING TIPS** Harvest the leaves of any kale variety as they grow, but note that as the plants mature, the leaves may become smaller and bitter. Grow kale from seed or seedling plants in late summer for a fall crop. In cool summer areas it can also be sown in spring for a summer harvest. The more heat-tolerant collards can be grown from fall into winter, or spring to summer.
- **COOKING TIPS** All can be steamed, stir-fried, added to soups and stews, or sautéed.

Brassica oleracea var. botrytis

cauliflower

Annual, sun, regular water

- **CUISINE** The difference between cauliflower and broccoli is slight, and probably best seen as a gradient from the tight green heads of broccoli through the ornate spirals of pale green broccoflower (romanesco) to cream-white cauliflower. The standard white heirloom cauliflower is 'Snowball Early'; 'Violeta Italia' is vivid purple when raw, turning bright green once cooked.
- **GROWING TIPS** White varieties must be protected from the sun by tying up their outer leaves around the developing heads. It must be cool during the months that it grows to reach maturity. Start seeds indoors about 7 weeks before the last frost. You can then transplant while the weather is still cool. Harvest as soon as the heads are firm; if you don't harvest promptly, individual heads become loose.
- **COOKING TIPS** All cauliflower varieties are sweet and tastier when cooked just after harvest, so growing your own is well worth it. The leaf, stalk, and florets can be eaten raw or cooked. Raw, it is eaten on its own or added to salads. When cooked, it can be eaten as a side dish or topped with a sauce, such as a classic cheese sauce.

Cichorium endiva

endive

Biennial, sun or light shade, moist

- **CUISINE** There are 3 main varieties of endive. Curly endive (sometimes mistakenly called chicory in the United States) has green, rimmed, curly outer leaves. Frisée has finely cut, frizzy leaves. Escarole has broad, pale green leaves and is less bitter than the other varieties.
- **GROWING TIPS** For a late spring harvest, seed 3 to 4 weeks before the last killing frost in spring. For an initial fall harvest, seed about 10 weeks before the first hard frost.
- **COOKING TIPS** Endive can be used raw in salads or cooked in a variety of ways, including stuffed, baked, boiled, steamed, or fried.

Cichorium intybus

chicory

Perennial, sun, water regularly

- **CUISINE** True chicory is a root vegetable whose green leafy tops are used as cooking greens or in salads. Roots of some varieties are also ground to make a coffee supplement, and others are forced in order to grow into French endive. The most well-known varieties are 'common chicory', 'Radichetta', 'Brunswick', and 'Magdeburg'.
- **GROWING TIPS** Sow seeds in the spring about 6 weeks after the last frost about ¼ inch (0.5 cm) deep and 3 inches (7.5 cm) apart.
- **COOKING TIPS** The very young leaves can be eaten fresh in salads and the older, bitter leaves can be boiled and eaten.

Eruca sativa (Diplotaxis tenuifolia)

arugula, wild arugula

Annual, sun, regular water

- **CUISINE** Also known as rocket (in England), roquette (France), and rucola or rughetta (Italy), these spicy greens are easy to grow throughout most of the season and are well adapted to green-house cultivation. Both have a peppery taste, with the wild arugula being the stronger.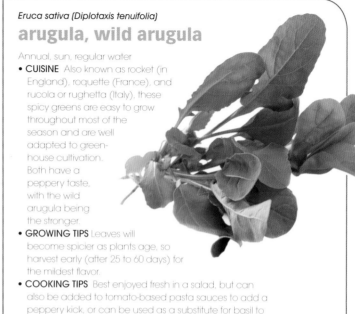
- **GROWING TIPS** Leaves will become spicier as plants age, so harvest early (after 25 to 60 days) for the mildest flavor.
- **COOKING TIPS** Best enjoyed fresh in a salad, but can also be added to tomato-based pasta sauces to add a peppery kick, or can be used as a substitute for basil to make an alternative pesto sauce.

Lactuca sativa

lettuce

Annual, full sun or partial shade, regular water

- **CUISINE** There are dozens of varieties of head and leaf lettuce, from the tender butter lettuce to crisp Romaine types.
- **GROWING TIPS** Lettuces are cool season annuals. They thrive when temperatures are around 60°F (15°C), but most varieties will flower, go to seed, and become bitter when the temperatures continue to rise. Sow seed outdoors as soon as the frosts have finished, and continue with successive plantings until summer. Sow fall crops after temperatures moderate. Lettuce may also be grown in cold frames or cool greenhouses over winter. Harvest baby lettuce leaves by snipping them off with scissors after 30 days, and take full heads from 65 days. Loose-leaf varieties are more widely grown in home gardens than heading types, because they are faster to mature, easier to grow, and more shade tolerant. Loose-leaf varieties of lettuce also require less thinning, and thrive under warmer conditions.
- **COOKING TIPS** The most obvious use for lettuce in the kitchen is as part of a salad. With such a huge variety of lettuce available, you can make wonderful salads of different colors, textures, and tastes. You can also use individual lettuce leaves as a wrap—as in Chinese restaurants, where lettuce encloses barbecued lamb or duck with hoisin or plum sauce. Lettuce leaves can be braised to serve with meat dishes, though some people find the texture of soft, warm lettuce unappealing. The large leaves of Butterhead lettuce are very useful in soups, either torn and stirred into the pot just before serving or placed in individual bowls with the soup added on top. The shredded leaves can also be added to stir-fries at the end of cooking.

Nasturtium officinale

watercress

Perennial grown as annual, full sun, moist

- **CUISINE** Watercress is another peppery green.
- **GROWING TIPS** Its natural habitat is along the edges of streams, so growing it in the garden requires diligent attention to its water requirements. The drier the conditions, the more concentrated the flavor will be. Sow seed after the frosts have finished, or sow in a cold frame for transplanting later. Begin harvesting after 30 days, and continue until the frosts strike or throughout the year in mild areas.
- **COOKING TIPS** Add the leaves to salads or sandwiches, and use to garnish meat dishes.

Spinacia oleracea

spinach

Annual, sun, regular water

- **CUISINE** True spinach is a cool-season annual.
- **GROWING TIPS** Harvest the young leaves by snipping them off with scissors after 30 days, or cut whole plants for a deeper flavor) after 50 days. In mild winter areas it can be sown as soon as temperatures are cool enough. In colder areas, it is best grown in a cold frame or as soon as the soil can be worked in spring.
- **COOKING TIPS** Spinach makes an excellent salad green, as well as being a versatile cooking green.

Tetragonia expansa

New Zealand spinach

Perennial, full sun, drought tolerant

- **CUISINE** New Zealand spinach, also known as sea spinach, has a flavor very similar to, but milder than, common spinach, but is a completely unrelated plant.
- **GROWING TIPS** A succulent evergreen in mild climates, it may go dormant in colder winters, and can be grown as a summer annual in the coldest regions. Harvest the young leaves and stems as they grow, and more shoots will appear within weeks. This versatile plant grows just about anywhere from cool, damp conditions, to sun and heat.
- **COOKING TIPS** A delicious substitute for spinach, the very young leaves and shoots can also be eaten raw in salads. However, they are best enjoyed cooked—use them cooked as you would normal spinach, but ensure that you use the young leaves, as older leaves can develop an acrid taste.

Valerianella locusta

corn salad

Annual, full sun, regular water

- **CUISINE** Also known as lamb's lettuce (because of its shape, reminiscent of a lamb's tongue) or mache, this mildly nutty green is a great addition to salads and has 3 times as much vitamin C as lettuce.
- **GROWING TIPS** It is a cool season crop and one of the hardiest. In warm climates, sow the seed from fall through to spring and harvest after about 90 days. In cold winter areas, sow as soon as the soil is workable for a spring harvest or through the summer for a fall harvest. Plants can reseed in mild areas, so leave several to flower. Harvest whole heads as they mature.
- **COOKING TIPS** Corn salad is used in salad mixes together with other greens such as mustard leaves, rocket, dandelion, frisee, etc. It can also be cooked like spinach, or used in soups and stuffings.

Baby vegetables

Vegetables that are grown and marketed as "baby vegetables" have become all the rage in upscale restaurants and markets. The vegetables are harvested before they reach full size and are served whole but, because they have not had time to fully develop, often have a more delicate taste than the mature kind.

An ever-increasing number of vegetables are available in baby varieties.

Most of these vegetables are annuals, growing quickly from seed to harvest. Since they are to be picked before they reach maturity, some, such as beets, radishes, leeks, and carrots, can be planted much closer together than normal. Another trick is to plant them thickly and then harvest some as babies, leaving the rest at their normal spacing to mature to full size. Baby vegetables can also be grown in pots, with one container full of carrots yielding a delicious meal of tender little roots. Sow a number of pots at intervals for a succession of servings.

Interestingly, some baby vegetables form after the main crop has been harvested. For example, small artichokes and diminutive broccoli spears (identical in flavor to the larger versions) form on the lower stem after the main crop has been cut off. There are also dwarf varieties of old favorites for adding interest to a gourmet meal. Eggplants, such as 'Hmong Red' and 'Goyo Kumba', are only 2–3 inches (5–7.5 cm) in diameter when fully grown. 'Little Finger' carrots grow to only 3 inches (7.5 cm) long, and 'Parmex' carrots are 1½–2 inches (3.6–5 cm) long and wide. Cherry-type tomatoes have been favorites for years, but there are even more diminutive varieties now. 'Red Currant' and 'Yellow Currant' are among the smallest tomatoes grown, with fruits less than ½ inch (12 mm) across, but still deliver a big tomato flavor.

Directory

Baby vegetables have grown in popularity over recent years, for their diminutive, but cute, appearance, flavorsome qualities, and ease of growth for the home gardener.

There are two distinct types of baby vegetables. The first kind are vegetables that have been grown closely together and harvested early to achieve the "baby" status. They are often quick-maturing varieties of vegetables—a good example being short-rooted carrots, such as Amsterdam Forcing, and King Richard leeks. The second group are also grown closely together, but have been bred specifically to stay small, and are actually dwarf varieties of the adult plant. Good examples of this are mini cauliflowers and cabbages.

The growth in popularity of baby vegetables, especially in the home gardening world, is mainly due to how easy it is to grow them. As mentioned above, they are often grown closely together, which makes them ideal for container gardening if you are short on space. They are also usually fast-maturing plants, which makes them perfect for the impatient gardener, and are ideal for getting quick results from your garden. However, because of this necessity for fast growth, it is imperative that you use good-quality compost and water them frequently to ensure the best progress.

Baby vegetables, as with all vegetables, are at their best when harvested, prepared, and cooked the same day—they are far superior to bought vegetables and a lot cheaper and easier to grow. For a continual supply of baby/mini vegetables, make successive sowings throughout the growing season. Harvest them as a young crop, when they are tender and full of flavor. It is also useful to grow vegetables of similar height next to each other to minimize shading of short vegetables by tall ones.

Allium ampeloprasum

leek

Annual, full sun, regular water
- **GROWING TIPS** The mild onion flavor of leeks is fully developed only after 3 months of growing, and harvesting them as baby leeks a month early will yield an even milder vegetable.
- **COOKING TIPS** Blanch or steam briefly and serve alone, or use to garnish scalloped potatoes or egg dishes.

Apium graveolens

celery

Annual, full sun, regular water
- **GROWING TIPS** Harvesting celery early can result in an even longer picking season. The stalks are picked when about 7 inches (18 cm) long when the flavor will be stronger than full-grown celery. Sow seed at twice the recommended rate in the garden, or grow in a pot for easy harvest.
- **COOKING TIPS** Braise or stir-fry whole with other vegetables to balance the flavor.

Beta vulgaris

beet

Annual, sun, regular water
- **GROWING TIPS** Baby beets are usually harvested when they are just 1 inch (2.5 cm) or so in diameter. Pull from the ground and wash thoroughly.
- **COOKING TIPS** Leave on a few of the leaves, steam briefly, and serve immediately. For even more color, combine red and golden beet on the same plate.

Spinacia oleracea

baby spinach

Annual, full sun to partial shade, regular water

- **GROWING TIPS** Protection from bad weather and cold is needed through winter. All leafy salads are ideal for planting in growing bags or in the greenhouse. Spinach prefers a well-draining soil and is a fast grower. Leaves are about 1–2 inches (25–50 mm) long.
- **COOKING TIPS** Baby spinach can be used in the same vein as the larger variety, but is best served raw to capitalize on the sweet, fresh flavor.

Brassica oleracea

Brussels sprouts

Annual, sun, regular water

- **GROWING TIPS** Baby Brussels sprouts are even better than their mature counterparts, with the strong cabbage flavor that can characterize the latter not having had time to develop.
- **COOKING TIPS** Mild and almost sweet, baby Brussels sprouts are well worth the effort. Start harvesting the buds before they reach 1 inch (2.5 cm) diameter. Steam or sauté briefly, and serve with butter or cheese sauce.

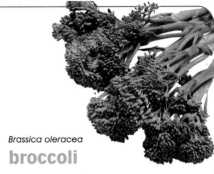

Brassica oleracea

broccoli

Annual, sun, regular water

- **GROWING TIPS** If you continue to nurture broccoli plants after the main harvest, they will generate a second batch of thin flower stems.
- **COOKING TIPS** They make good baby vegetables and are prepared whole like the large spears. Steam or sauté briefly to retain their crispness and color. Seasoned with Asian spices, drizzled with balsamic vinegar, or sprinkled with grated cheese they can be included in meals from many different parts of the world.

Brassica oleracea

cauliflower

Annual, sun, regular water

- **GROWING TIPS** Baby cauliflowers are harvested when they are about 4 inches (10 cm) in diameter. In commercial fields, this will be only about 10 days before the regular harvest. The immature flower heads are tight and tender.
- **COOKING TIPS** Steam whole or bake in a casserole smothered in cheese sauce.

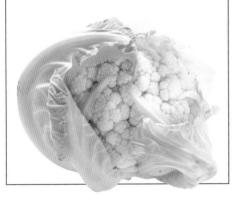

Brassica rapa*

turnips

Annual, sun, regular water

- **GROWING TIPS** Sow in the spring when the soil can be worked in an area that has not been manured. Harvest by gently pulling out by the bottoms of the greens. Baby turnips come in yellow-, orange-, red-, and white-fleshed varieties.
- **COOKING TIPS** Turnips are great munched whole, in salads, or steamed and dressed with butter. Turnip greens are mild, so they can be eaten raw in salads—treat them as you would radishes.

Brassica rapa

bok choy

Annual, sun, regular water

- **GROWING TIPS** There are many varieties of Chinese cabbage, and many that go under the name of bok choy (or pak choi). All are suitable for harvesting at an early stage and serving whole as a baby vegetable.
- **COOKING TIPS** Since the flavor is delicate and the crisp stems are full of water, cook gently. Add the whole rosette to soups or blanch briefly, then heat in oil or butter to which garlic, ginger, or a dash of oyster sauce has been added.

Cucurbita pepo

summer squash

Annual, full sun, regular water

- **GROWING TIPS** All the tender-skinned squashes, such as zucchini, patty pan, and the crookneck types, can be harvested when very young to serve whole. Often they will still have the flowers attached to provide even more interest. If you've ever had to keep up with a prolific zucchini plant, harvesting squashes at this stage will seem like a true blessing. Act promptly or they'll turn into baseball bat-sized fruits.
  - **COOKING TIPS** Steam briefly or drop into tempura batter and fry quickly. Baby squashes may also be coated with oil and grilled. Just give a few turns to heat them through and give nice scorch marks.

Cucurbita sativus

cucumber

- **GROWING TIPS** Baby cucumbers can be anywhere between 2.5 and 7 inches (6 and 18 cm) long and are medium green colored, with a firm, crisp texture.
- **COOKING TIPS** Their crisp, tasty flavor makes baby cucumbers ideal as a snack cucumber, perfect in salads, and lend themselves well to pickling.

Cynara scolymus

artichoke

Perennial, full to part sun, regular water

- **GROWING TIPS** Artichokes produce more flower buds after the main one has been harvested at full size. These secondary buds—the baby artichokes—will never attain the size of that central one. Pick them when they are just 1 inch (2.5 cm) or so in diameter when they will not have much, if any, of the "choke" and can be eaten whole.
- **COOKING TIPS** Steam or grill, and serve with melted butter or mayonnaise.

Daucus carota

carrot

Annual, sun, regular water

- **GROWING TIPS** This root vegetable is among the sweetest when harvested very young. Pull carrots when they are only 3–4 inches (7.5–10 cm) long.
- **COOKING TIPS** Wash, leave the ferny leaves, and steam briefly. Commercial baby carrots without the tops are often just regular carrots that have been cut down to size. By growing your own, you will have the authentic, delicious baby vegetable.

Latuca sativa

lettuce

Annual, full to part sun, regular water

- **GROWING TIPS** Because of the huge variety of lettuces available these are perfect when picked young to accentuate the flavor. Best sown thickly and clipped young for baby leaves. Sow every 2 weeks for a continuous supply of tender young lettuce leaves.
- **COOKING TIPS** Wash thoroughly before use. Perfect in a salad with other baby vegetables, such as baby spinach and tomatoes.

Lycopersicon esculentum

tomato

Annual, full sun, regular water

- **GROWING TIPS** With names like 'Cuban Grape' (yellow orange), 'Coyote' (cream-white), and 'Black Cherry' (nearly black shade of red), there are miniature tomatoes of every color. They are also among the tastiest tomatoes, the small size seeming to result in concentrated goodness. Baby tomatoes are also well suited to growing in containers. Easy to harvest, they can even be grown in hanging baskets and are also perfect for a child's first garden.

Phaseolus vulgaris

green beans or haricots verts

Annual, sun, regular water

- **GROWING TIPS** There are some varieties of green beans that have been developed specifically for uniform crops of haricot verts. Any variety, when harvested at an immature stage, will yield tender, baby green beans. Pick often to capture the delicate flavor and uniform size.
- **COOKING TIPS** Toss raw into salads, marinate in mild vinaigrette, or steam quickly and dress with butter.

Pisum sativum

peas

Annual, sun, regular water

- **GROWING TIPS** French gardeners have long grown these fine shelling peas (*petits pois*), which are harvested while the peas are small but intensely sweet. Pick peas frequently for a tender, sweet crop of baby shoots. Because of their small size, they are perfect for container growing and shouldn't need any support, generally growing about 17.5 inches (45 cm) high.
- **COOKING TIPS** Can be used in much the same way as their adult variety, but are best cooked quickly to retain their sweetness.

Solanum melongena

eggplant

Annual, full sun, regular water

- **GROWING TIPS** Many varieties of eggplant are naturally small. Although it is possible to harvest larger varieties before they reach full size, be sure to leave them until they develop their characteristic color or they will be tasteless and uninteresting.
- **COOKING TIPS** Most commonly used in Thai curries. The whole vegetable can be used in cooking, but use it carefully, as this dwarf variety can sometimes be bitter.

Solanum tuberosum

potato

Grown as annual, full sun, water regularly

- **GROWING TIPS** There are some varieties of potatoes, like fingerling potatoes, that are naturally small. They are generally 1–2 inches (2.5–5 cm) in diameter and less than 5 inches (13 cm) long. They come in several skin colors, from pink to purple, tan, and nearly white. For a clean, easy harvest, grow potatoes on top of the soil and mound clean mulch, such as straw, around the plant as it grows. Gently pull the mulch away from the plant to pick the potatoes, and then tuck the plant back in to continue growing. The nice thing about harvesting a few new potatoes in early spring is that the plant will continue to grow and produce more tubers for several months. New potatoes are the true babies. They are harvested when very young from 1 to 3 inches (2.5 to 7.5 cm) in diameter, just when the plant begins to flower.
- **COOKING TIPS** The skin will be very tender and the flavor sweet. Because storage of a potato of any size leads to a thickened skin and increased starch levels, rush them to the kitchen for the best flavor. All are firm and suitable for any manner of cooking from boiling to roasting.

Zea mays

corn

Annual, full sun, regular water

- **GROWING TIPS** Baby corn varieties are naturally smaller, but they are also grown more intensively to force the plant to make smaller cobs. Look for the likes of 'Minor F1 Hybrid' and sow seed at twice the recommended rate. Harvest the tiny corn before pollination, just as the silk tassels begin to show.
- **COOKING TIPS** Blanch and add to soups or stews. They are excellent with seafood, or stir-fried with other tender vegetables.

Mushrooms

There is no substitute for the earthy goodness of mushrooms. They lend their aroma and unique texture to the likes of sauces, stews, and egg dishes. There are an increasing number of sources of fungal inoculums, and a myriad of ways to grow these fungal wonders that add their particular texture and earthy flavor to all sorts of dishes.

Mushroom hunting is not for the faint of heart and requires an excellent knowledge of what the edible ones look like; mushroom poisoning can cause severe gastrointestinal pain and even death, so most people prefer to buy them. If you are worried about making the call between safe and sorry, growing your own from commercially developed spores can be a good way to bring the flavor of woodland mushrooms into the kitchen.

Just one or two types of edible mushroom used to be available at the market, and even when mushroom-growing kits appeared, they were likely to be for the ubiquitous *Agaricus bisporus*. This is the very familiar white-capped mushroom still found in everything from pizzas to cream of mushroom soup. Now it's possible to have a wide variety of fresh fungi, not only from the market, but for growing yourself. Although dried mushrooms certainly retain all the flavor of the fresh kind, the texture never fully recovers on soaking. Growing them at home allows you to harvest them at peak freshness and have the best flavor and texture instantly available.

Mushrooms are used to add texture and flavor to a dish. They are now recognized as an important part of a healthy diet.

Growing mushrooms

With a growing kit, anyone can grow edible fungi both indoors and outdoors. Plastic bags, paper, and wood are all suitable media for growing your own delicious range of mushrooms.

Mushroom kits

The revolution in growing mushrooms commercially is testimony to the growers' increasing knowledge about how to coax them to thrive in an artificial setting. And now that knowledge has spilled into the realm of the amateur. Mushroom-growing kits, spawn, and other paraphernalia are readily available for many species.

What are mushrooms?

Mushrooms are the reproductive structures of a fungus. Most of the time the vegetative body of the fungus lives unseen as extremely thin filaments spread through the growing medium. This medium is usually specific for each type (e.g., wood or dung), and provides the carbon the fungi need. The fungi digest the medium by releasing powerful enzymes to break it down—that's why it's tricky growing them out of their natural environment.

Planters

The simplest kits will probably look like a plastic bag stuffed full of straw or sawdust, with holes punched through the plastic film. These have been sown with the spores of a particular species, and you just dampen the kit according to the directions and maintain it at the optimum temperature for that species. Within weeks to months, depending on the species, the mycelium will have grown outward and mushrooms will sprout from the holes. You pluck them off as they appear and head for the kitchen. The leftover medium can often be coaxed to continue fruiting if given an additional source of carbon. You can stuff it into the cracks of a log or sprinkle it at the edge of a mulch or compost pile and hope that the mycelium finds its way into the new medium.

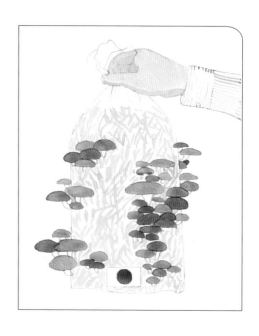

Logs

Once you are hooked on growing your own mushrooms, try growing them outdoors. Many—such as oyster and shiitake mushrooms—grow well on wood. Manufacturers have developed ways of inoculating a small, sawdust-based plug with mycelium. The plugs are stuffed into holes drilled in freshly cut logs or treestumps. The logs are stored for one to two years to allow the mycelium to grow into the length of the wood. Temperature changes in spring and autumn trigger the growth of the spores into fully fruited mushrooms; or you can kickstart this process by soaking the logs in water. Once established, a mushroom log will continue sprouting for many years, until the whole of the wood becomes decomposed.

1 Place the "plug" spawn in a suitable log (hardwoods such as oak, cottonwood and elm are often recommended). Holes can be painted with beeswax to protect the mycelium during incubation. The ends of the logs can also be painted with wax if moisture retention is a concern.

2 After 12 months of incubation, the logs are checked for mycelia growth by chipping away an area of bark around one of the plugs. If mycelia growth is evident, fruiting is initiated by soaking the logs by submerging them in a tub or tank (or watering with a sprinkler) for 24 hours.

Drying mushrooms

Many mushroom varieties—particularly ceps and morels—retain their flavor and texture when dried and reconstituted; in fact, the flavor of ceps is noticeably enhanced by the drying process. Drying mushrooms at home is an easy way to extend their shelf life. Buy the freshest, firmest mushrooms available. Halve and clean them. Either heat them gently in a commercial dehydrator or domestic oven—at no higher than 120°F (49°C), for around 6 hours—or thread the pieces onto long strings and hang from the kitchen ceiling. Once dried in this manner, and stored in an airtight container, the mushrooms will remain edible for up to 2 years.

Paperback books

Growing your own mushrooms is possible even if you have only a compact space. You'll need to choose the variety of mushroom carefully, as not all are suitable for this method: Oyster mushrooms would be an ideal choice.

Reconstituting and using dried mushrooms

Most dried mushrooms can be reconstituted simply by immersing them in boiling water for 10 minutes. They are then ready for cooking—to be stirred into a risotto, stir-fried with Chinese vegetables, or whatever other method you choose. If you have time, and can remember to think ahead, your mushrooms will have a deeper, richer flavor if soaked for a longer period (overnight at best) in cold water.

1 Take a fairly thick paperback book, and soak it in hot water. Spread the contents of a packet of mushroom spores at regular intervals throughout the damp pages. Seal the book inside a polythene bag.

2 Keep it in a warm place, exposed to indirect sunlight, watering it daily with a plant mister. When the spores begin to grow, move the bag to a cool spot until the mushrooms are fully grown (this will take a total of around 2–3 weeks).

Directory

Beyond the humble white-capped mushroom, edible fungi come in an amazing array of shapes, tastes, and textures—each variety suited to a different type of cuisine.

Homegrown mushrooms add an earthy, yet exotic, element to the gourmet garden. Invaluable additions to soups, stews, and pasta dishes, their culinary uses extend into the realms of pizza toppings, salads, stir-fries, and more. Stuffed, they are a meal in themselves, or served up on buttered toast provide a simple but satisfying snack.

Given their range of shapes and textures, it is not surprising that different types of fungi are more suited to certain types of cuisine. Portobellos, delicate enokis, and pretty lavender-blue blewitts are all suitable for eating raw in salads. Of those listed here, oyster mushrooms are the only ones that should never be eaten raw, as this can interfere with the digestive process. The shapes of portobellos and, especially, the hollow morels lend themselves to being stuffed with bread crumbs or—for

carnivores—sausage meat. For vegetarians, large portobellos can be an excellent meat substitute, and morels perfectly complement pasta, risotto, egg dishes, and, in particular, the irresistably delicate flavor of asparagus. With their good looks and full flavor, shiitake mushrooms are all-round winners, lending themselves to almost any type of culinary preparation. And by growing your own, you will have access to button shiitakes, a form rarely seen at markets.

In the wild, mushrooms sprout up in damp, woodland places. Mushroom-growing kits replicate these conditions with sawdust, paper, and logs, and a requirement for cool, dark indoor growing conditions. Morels can be grown out of doors, but you will have to be patient—they can take as long as 2 years to produce.

Agaricus bisporus

portobello or cremini

Portobellos are just a very large version of the cremini (or baby bella) mushroom, and are a wilder relative of the common white mushroom. Pick them small as baby bellas, or allow them to expand and open to the familiar 4-inch (10-cm) portobellos.

- **COOKING TIPS** The small, tight buttons are perfect when served whole, either raw in salads or sautéed, or roasted with meats. Pick the two-bite-sized creminis to stuff as an appetizer, or use the large portobellos as a meat substitute by broiling to serve whole or thinly sliced with a savory sauce.
- **GROWING TIPS** Easy to grow and very productive, portobello kits will produce a flush every 10–14 days until the medium is exhausted.

Fammulina velutipes

enokitake or enoki

The delicate enokitake mushrooms grow in dense clusters of pale thread-like stems topped with tiny rounded caps. The most unmushroomy mushroom, enokitakes are very delicate in flavor and texture.

- **COOKING TIPS** They are at their best when tossed in salads, used to garnish meat dishes, or stirred into tasty broth-based soups.
- **GROWING TIPS** In the wild they grow on wood, but commercial kits may contain sawdust, rice bran, and corncob meal. They prefer very cool temperatures— 40–60°F (4–16°C)—to thrive.

Lentinula edodes and *Lentinus edodes*

shiitake

First cultivated in China as long ago as 960 A.D., it took another thousand years or more for shiitake to come into production in the United States. The robust flavor and handsome dark color are universally popular. But here's why growing your own actually yields a premium product that is rarely available in markets: the button shiitake.

• **COOKING TIPS** These tight little unopened mushrooms have the best flavor and texture, and both characteristics stand up to almost any preparation. Use only the caps (keep the stems for making tasty broths) with vegetables, grains, greens, and meats.

• **GROWING TIPS** A shiitake kit can produce 2–3 pounds (0.9–1.4 kg) of mushrooms over a 12–16-week period.

Lepista nuda

blewitt

One of the most colorful and tastiest mushrooms, blewitts are pale lavender to bluish. They are large, sturdy mushrooms that typically appear in spring in the wild. Although seldom available in markets, they can be grown from commercially inoculated media that can be mixed with compost outdoors.

• **COOKING TIP** In the kitchen treat them like portobello mushrooms.

Morchella spp.

morel

Although the taste is no more special than any other mushroom, the crinkly morel has long been sought after, which is why new techniques and cultures have been developed to help people grow it.

• **COOKING TIPS** Because morels are hollow, they are ideal for stuffing; sauté or roast with oil, then slice in half and fill with sausage or bread-crumb stuffing. The flavor also goes well with cream and egg dishes, pasta, risotto, and, particularly, asparagus.

• **GROWING TIPS** Unlike many of the other mushrooms mentioned here, morels can be cultivated outdoors from commercially available spores (also called spawn). Success may depend as much on luck as on diligence, but many people have profited by trying. Morels may fruit at any time of the year, but spring is typical. Your patch may take 2 years to produce any mushrooms, so cultivate patience as well.

Pleurotus spp.

oyster

Oyster mushrooms come in a wide array of colors, including pink, yellow, blue, and near black. The most commonly grown one is pale white, turning to buff on the off-center caps. All grow in clusters with caps forming on one side of the stalk, or, if the stalks are extremely short, they may appear as shelves.

• **COOKING TIPS** Very mild in flavor, they are valued because they mop up the flavor of other ingredients or sauces. This is one of the few mushrooms that is good for roasting; coat it with oil and cook quickly at high heat to improve the texture and bring out flavor.

• **GROWING TIPS** The flavor of oyster mushrooms is among the least tantalizing, but different media will produce more intensity. Those grown on straw will be the mildest, whereas wood gives a robust taste. Do not eat raw: Oyster mushrooms contain compounds (broken down in cooking) that can interfere with digestion.

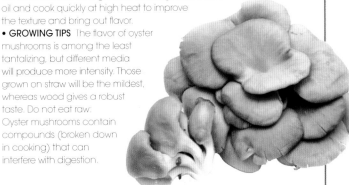

Fruit

Eating sweet and succulent fruit, fresh from your own garden, is one of the greatest joys of growing your own food. You'll never go back to bland and pallid commercial varieties after picking your homegrown produce.

There are lots of good reasons to grow your own fruit and vegetables. Fruit that travels long distances from farm to market has to be picked before it is fully ripe, and this means it won't have peaked in color and taste. And the diversity of available varieties is much greater than you will find in local stores.

Growing your own also makes good financial sense. Over the life of a fruit tree (50 years or more), you will have saved the cost of buying a similar amount of produce many times over. And, with careful culture, self-renewing berries can survive for decades as well. In addition, when you grow and harvest your own food, you control the means of treating pests and adding fertility to the soil. This is particularly true of long-lived plants, such as trees and perennial berries, which you want to keep in good health for years. But one of the most satisfying aspects is being able to pick fruit when it's at the peak of flavor, far surpassing what store-bought fruit tastes like.

There is a never-ending variety of fruit to choose from for your home garden—you won't fail to find something to please your whole family.

Fruit trees

There's no longer any need to confine your fruit picking to the local pick-your-own orchard—many, many fruits are more than suitable for the home garden, and will provide you with a ready supply of tasty fruit all year-round.

THINNING FRUIT

When the trees are producing a good crop, you'll need to thin the fruit before it matures. This channels the tree's limited resources to fewer fruits so that they can grow larger. Look at each branch and remove most of the clustered fruits, saving just one per branch. Also make sure that the fruits are spaced along the Branch at about 6-inch (15-cm) intervals.

Planting

For most of the deciduous fruit trees (and berries), the best time to plant is during the fall to winter dormant period. Many plants spend weeks or months in a state of suspended animation through the cold winter months. Gardeners and farmers have discovered that this is an ideal time to dig up the plants and move them around without adversely interfering with their growth. Nurseries offer bare-root trees in winter that can be half the cost (or less) of the same species grown in a pot. One great advantage in planting bare-root specimens is that you can put their roots directly into your existing soil. There will be no problems associated with having one soil type in the pot and another in your plot.

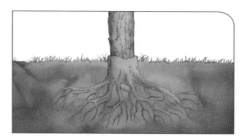

1 When digging the planting hole make it at least twice as wide as the diameter of the roots, and a little bit deeper. Hold the plant upright in place in the hole, and shovel the soil back around the roots. Be sure to poke it in around all of them.

2 Make sure that the soil level is exactly where it was before the plant was dug up. Many fruit trees have been grafted onto a different rootstock, and you can clearly see that union. The graft line should remain just above the soil.

3 It is often helpful to create a small berm around the planting hole to help channel water to the roots of the young tree. Fill the basin several times with water to settle the soil. Also add a woody mulch, and renew it regularly.

Preparation

Always plant immediately, but if you can't, protect the roots by placing them in a bag filled with damp sand, peat moss, or compost. An overnight soak in water can help, but don't soak it for more than this, because the roots need oxygen even in the dormant state. The addition of vitamin B to the solution is also recommended, but there's no argument about the positive effects from using mycorrhizae. These microscopic fungi form a beneficial symbiotic relationship with new roots, and increase their ability to support the plant (both the vitamin and mycorrhizae are available from nurseries).

Dwarf varieties

Since most of the available fruit cultivars don't grow as well on their native roots, they will have been grafted onto a variety of other rootstocks. The type of rootstock used influences the ultimate size and vigor of the tree, the timing of fruit production, its adaptability, and resistance to disease. Your nursery will most likely have made this rootstock choice for you, but some will give you a selection. When you purchase a "dwarf" tree, it will have been grafted onto rootstock that reduces its overall size from as much as 30 feet (9 m) to 8 feet (2.4 m). "Semi-dwarfs" will be somewhere in the middle, usually about 12–25 feet (3.6–7.5 m) high. "Mini" varieties won't exceed 5 feet (1.5 m) for growing in a container.

For gardeners with limited space the dwarf trees are an important option. Ease in picking fruit and the possibility of planting more varieties are advantages. Other alternatives include planting more than one tree of the same vigor in the same hole, pruning to maintain size, training espalier trees along walls, and planting multiple-budded trees. The tree might have different types of peach or apple grafted onto a single root system, or could have a peach, plum, and apricot all on the same tree.

CROSS-POLLINATION

Many fruit trees are self-fertile, meaning that the pollen from their flowers is capable of fertilizing their own ovaries. But in some cases (most apples and pears, and some plums) a different plant is required to provide the pollen. If a pollinator is needed, the plant's label will indicate this and usually suggest one or more likely varieties that bloom at the same time. If you have room for several trees, choose varieties with staggered blooming and ripening times to extend the picking season.

Choosing your fruit tree

Examine your prospective purchases carefully, first for healthy roots. Usually nurseries will display plants in communal bins filled with moist organic material or sand. The roots should be plump and flexible, not shriveled and brittle. Some may have been damaged either in the digging-up process or in transit. If every root has some damage, and pruning it all off leaves you with lots of little stubs, forget it. When you get your plants home, cut off any of those broken ends with sharp shears to minimize the surface area open to disease or infection. Also double-check your nursery's guarantee policy. Most will replace the plant if you find it deficient, but there will be a time limit, usually one year or one season.

The next thing to look for is healthy above-ground growth. A tree will most likely be a single, thin "whip" (although it may have one or two very small branches, depending on how old it is) rising from the roots. Again, check that it is plump and flexible, not wrinkled or brittle, and that the tender bark is undamaged without abrasions. The top of the stem doesn't matter too much because you will be pruning it back. When planting, cut it back by about one-quarter to one-third of the total height, typically 38–42 inches (91–107 cm), leaving plenty of dormant buds for later development.

Pruning

Good pruning is vital in the success of home gardening fruit trees—keep on top of it and your trees should supply you with a constant source of fruit for many, many years.

Pruning for success

The general goals are to open up the tree for good light penetration and encourage a strong branch structure to support the fruit without breaking. There are two main types of structure to choose from when starting with a young tree—a central leader type or a vase-like structure. Some fruits respond better to one than the other. Apples, cherries, and pears are successful if pruned to a central leader, whereas peaches and nectarines do best as vase shapes. Plums and apricots can go either way.

WHEN TO PRUNE

Winter, after their leaves have fallen, is the time to prune deciduous fruit trees. It affords an opportunity to improve the structure while the plants are dormant. Cuts made to branches during this season direct the growth that begins again in spring. It is the prime time to shape fruit trees for health and productivity.

Central leader type

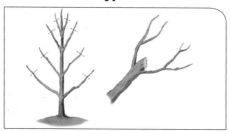

1 Trees with a central leader have a single trunk supporting ranks of branches. In the first year, the whip is cut down by about one third. It will then form several sets of branches below that cut.

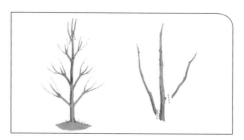

2 The next year, choose the central leader by removing one or more of the branches at the top, leaving just the single, upright one.

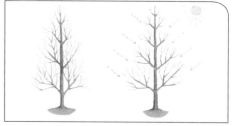

3 In subsequent years, thin the ranks so that they are evenly spaced around the central leader and alternating above each other. Rremember that you are attempting to let the maximum light strike all the branches.

Vase shape

1 To encourage a vase shape, the central leader is removed and lower branches are encouraged, providing what is known as the scaffold. Cut the whip to 30–42 inches above the soil level at planting.

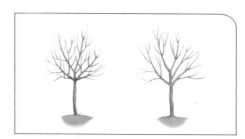

2 During the next years, the 3 to 5 scaffold branches will be developed by thinning the side branches these scaffold branches produce.

3 The result is a vase or basket of several strong radiating limbs with a network of smaller, fruit-bearing wood.

How to do it

Cuts should always be made at an angle of about 45 degrees, never perpendicular to the direction of growth. When removing entire branches, whatever their size, make the cuts as close to the main branch as possible without affecting the branch's cambium layer just under the bark. If stubs are left, they are subject to danger of fungal attack. The result of these cuts is the growth of new branches from the bud or buds below the cut either on the same branch or the one directly below it. This occurs because the growing tip has been producing a plant growth hormone that retards the growth of lower buds. When it is removed, these buds are released from their dormancy. Besides the rule of never leaving a stub, the next rule of pruning is to use sharp tools, either hook-and-blade shears or pruning saws. Sharp tools will leave clean cuts that heal faster and better with less possibility of insect or disease entry through the cut surface. Most experts now agree that painting these cut surfaces with a sealer is not necessary and in fact may retard the growth of necessary callus. Once the basic shape of the tree has been developed, the work of pruning each year is fairly simple. The first task is to find and remove any dead wood. Then look for any branches that cross each other. Remove or head them back so that they produce growth toward the outside of the tree. Future branching comes from dormant buds below the growing tip of the branch, so make cuts above buds that are on the outside, or bottom, of the branch. These will then grow in the next season in the desired direction.

Fruit-specific tips

Apples tend to grow very upright branches. More fruit will develop if branches can be made to spread out from the tree. When the branches are young, spread them apart with small pieces of lath or other wood. Fruit develops on short spurs in most varieties, so cut long whips to encourage the short side branches.

Pears usually need little pruning, and too much may induce production of lots of weak shoots.

Peaches and nectarines produce fruit on 1-year-old wood, so prune out more than you would other fruit trees to ensure that there is always plenty of new growth. The scaffold branches also respond to shortening if you want to keep the tree at a reasonable height.

Plums tend to produce long suckers or whips if pruned heavily. Lightly thin out to promote shorter spurs.

Apricots definitely need annual pruning to keep the tree open. They, too, need to have plenty of new growth for fruit production.

DON'T FORGET

...that small mistakes in pruning can be corrected in future years. Healthy trees respond with renewed vigor when carefully trained and pruned.

Fruit Trees Directory

Thankfully the days of needing acres of land to grow fruit are long gone—now all you need is some garden space and a bit of research into the most suitable fruit trees for your climate and location.

There's a fruit tree for every space and they aren't difficult to grow. You do need to follow a few ground rules to achieve success, however: The tree has to suit the climate, the position in the garden, and, most important, the soil. Healthy soil is imperative for good tree growth and fruit.

Patience is the key—although it takes a few years for the trees to begin to bear fruit, you will be rewarded with a bountiful supply of fruit for 20 to 50 years in the future. As you wait for your fruit tree to mature, there are some things that you can do to help it along: Maintain mulch around the base of the tree, fertilize it with any lawn fertilizer in the spring and in the fall, and protect its tender, emerging branches from deer, mice, and other wildlife (as well as the family dog).

In the spring of the second year your tree may produce some flowers which, if left on, would develop into fruit. It is better to pinch these flowers off and let the tree have another full year to develop its root system. A stronger, hardier tree will be your reward.

Once your tree begins to bear fruit, you will want to continue with the maintenance as you have been doing. In addition, you may find you need to spray it occasionally with a fruit tree spray if bugs are a problem. Once your fruit gets to be about the size of your thumbnail, you may want to thin it out, as the fruit that grows closely in clusters will not reach a good size. Other than that you can sit back and wait for your fruit to ripen.

Malus spp.

apple

Deciduous, full sun, regular water

- **CUISINE** By choosing carefully for your climate zone, it is possible to have apples ripening from midsummer to late fall. If space is at a premium, there are also grafted trees that contain two or three different varieties on a single trunk.
- **VARIETIES** Crispy, juicy, versatile apples have a long history of cultivation. The result is an amazing number of different varieties. A few to look out for: For a sweet fruit, try 'Honeycrisp'; for a tart fruit, try 'Granny Smith'; for a crisp fruit, try 'Macoun'; and for pie-making try 'Northern Spy', 'Liberty' apple trees, and 'Golden Delicious'.
- **GROWING TIPS** Apples bear fruit on short spurs that grow from wood that is 2 years old or more. Training apple trees into a pyramid shape is standard practice, but they can also be espaliered to save space. Cross-pollination is a good idea with apple growing. For example you could plant a 'Granny Smith' apple tree and a 'Macintosh' apple tree, and have enough wonderful apples to eat, cook with, make applesauce from, and share with your neighbors. Even trees that are marketed as being self-pollinating usually do better when more than one variety is planted, producing more and larger fruit.
    The best test of when an apple is ready to eat is to sample one—if it tastes good, it's ready. Another method is to take the apple in the palm of your hand and give it a slight twist—if it drops off, it is probably ready to eat.

When harvesting apples, take care not to bruise them—this will cause them to rot much more quickly, and if in storage, the rot will spread to other apples.

- **COOKING TIPS** Apples are famous for their keeping abilities. With cool storage, the fruit remains delicious and edible for many months.

Prunus armeniaca

apricot

Deciduous, full sun, regular water

- **CUISINE** Originating in China, apricots have spread throughout the world. Their dense flesh is both tart and sweet, and the ease of splitting the fruit and discarding the loose pit makes them ideal for eating from the hand. Apricot trees can be a lovely centerpiece in a yard: Their blossoms are white or pink; their foliage is bronze in the spring, deep green in the summer, and yellow in the fall.
- **VARIETIES** When choosing a variety, select one recommended for your climate that will flower after the last spring frost and that will live through the winter. The full-size trees generally grow between 20 and 30 feet (6 and 9 m) tall and live about 75 years. Most will start bearing in their third or fourth year. Expect 3 to 4 bushels of fruit from a standard-size tree, 1 to 2 from a dwarf variety.
- **GROWING TIPS** Since apricots bloom early (when the days are still relatively short), they are not usually successful in areas where late frosts occur. Most varieties also require more winter chill than many sub-tropical and Mediterranean climate zones can supply. Prune to allow sunlight into the interior of the tree for greater fruit production. Because of the threat of silver leaf, pruning should be avoided during winter months when this fungus produces most of its spores. Apricots must mature on the tree, but they can ripen either on or off the tree. If left until they are good to eat, they will bruise very easily with picking and transport.
- **COOKING TIPS** Apricots are delicious in pies and other confections; they make excellent jam and can even be added to meat stews, such as the tagines of Morocco, to enrich their flavor.

Pyrus communis, P. pyrifolia, and P. ussuriensis hybrids

European pear, Asian pear

Deciduous, full sun, regular water

- **CUISINE** The 2 edible types of pear are worlds apart in texture, but have similar flavors. European pears combine juiciness and a velvety texture with the characteristic gritty cells for perfect sweet salads and desserts. They are picked when firm, but eaten at a soft, ripe stage. Asian pears never achieve that softness and are usually eaten raw in salads or as an appetizer.
- **VARIETIES** Most varieties require a different pollinator. Conference is the most commonly grown because it withstands unfavorable conditions. Doyenne de Comice are judged by many to have the best taste—but this pear is a bit temperamental and appreciates a protected, warm position.
- **GROWING TIPS** Both types of pear should be grown as pyramids, and the fruit is produced on short spurs that continue to be productive for many years. Pear trees should be pruned annually in winter when they are dormant. Since both types are picked when firm, care should be taken to harvest when they are ripe. Ripe fruit will snap off the branch easily when you lift it; if it doesn't come off easily, it is not ready. Pick them when the flesh begins to change color around the stalk and store for a week before eating.

- **COOKING TIPS** In addition to being served raw in almost anything, pears can be baked, poached, sautéed, roasted, and grilled. They can be used as an ingredient in baked goods, and can be made into preserves.

Prunus domestica

plum

Deciduous, full sun, regular water

- **CUISINE** Plums come in many colors. The skin may be nearly black, blue, purple, red, green, or yellow, and the flesh ranges from green to yellow, orange, and deep red. All are juicy and sweet, perfect when eaten raw, but also wonderful in many baked dishes and preserves. Prunes are the sweetest of the lot, with a sugar content nearly twice that of the others and thus very suitable for drying.
- **VARIETIES** Taxonomists divide plums into 2 or 3 different groups. For home growers, you only need find the varieties that suit your climate. There are lots to choose from, but note many plums need another variety to pollinate them. The bullace is strictly a cooking plum. The trees are smaller than normal and very hardy, they are also ornamental. The fruit has a very sharp flavor, excellent for jellies and preserving. Damsons are another cooking plum, but sweeter than the bullace. The fruits have a sharpish taste and are ideal for pies, tarts, and jellies. Gages are eating (dessert) plums—they are the sweetest type of plum and have a distinct fragrance. Victoria plums are a popular variety with large fruits and an excellent taste. The flesh is green to yellow and very juicy.
- **GROWING TIPS** Plums make many long shoots each year and need heavy pruning to shorten and thin them out. They also require diligent thinning of the young fruit to increase the size of the harvested plums, and reduce the likelihood of breaking wood. Plum trees love full sun and a well-drained soil. If spring frosts are a concern, plant the tree in a sunny, sheltered area and avoid planting in an area where frost may settle and damage the blossoms.

    In general plums are a tree that can spread up to 20 feet (6 m) wide and 20 feet (6 m) tall. A standard plum tree will yield up to 3 bushels of plums. Smaller dwarf varieties will provide approximately 1 bushel of plums and semi-dwarf plum trees 2 bushels.

Prunus persica and *P. nucipersica*

peach and nectarine

Deciduous, full sun, regular water

- **CUISINE** Fuzzy peaches and their smooth-skinned relatives, nectarines, are the largest of the stone fruits, often the size of a baseball. They are juicy and range in flavor from tart to sugary. Nothing can compare to a ripe peach and, fortunately, they are among the few fruits that can be picked a few days before they are fully ripe, being allowed to ripen in the kitchen without losing too much flavor. Unfortunately, commercially grown peaches and nectarines are picked well before that point and never achieve their full flavor.
- **VARIETIES** Peach flowers are self-fruitful. Therefore, it is not necessary to plant more than one peach variety in the backyard. Choose your variety of tree based on your planned usage for the fruit— some types are best for canning and cooking, whereas others taste best fresh from the branch.
- **GROWING TIPS** Peaches and nectarines need more extensive pruning than most fruit trees. They are best trained into a vase shape. Since they flower and fruit on 1-year-old branches, as much as two-thirds of the wood will need to be removed each year.
- **COOKING TIPS** The flesh of peaches and nectarines will darken with exposure to air, so they must be cooked or eaten immediately once cut or further treated. Although the fuzzy skin is perfectly edible, it becomes tough when cooked. To remove the skin, blanch in boiling water for 1 minute and then immediately plunge into cold water to cease the cooking process. The skin should easily slip off.

Prunus L.

cherry

Deciduous, full sun, regular water
- **CUISINE** Small, sweet cherries are normally enjoyed raw, though they are sometimes made into a sauce for serving with duck or game.
- **VARIETIES** Most varieties are sweet—they have a thick, rich, almost plumlike texture and sweet taste. Sour cherry varieties are also called pie cherries. Although sweet and sour cherries have very similar growing requirements and are subject to the same pests, tart cherries are more tolerant of cold winters and long, hot, humid summers and have fewer disease problems.
- **GROWING TIPS** Almost all cherry varieties require a long chilling, and perform best in zones with plenty of frost. Most also require another variety to pollinate their flowers, so choose your varieties carefully. Growing cherry trees will guarantee a huge bird population flocking to your garden. If you want to eat the cherries, you will have to guard against the birds—they can strip a tree in less than half an hour.

  Choose a sunny site with good air circulation and deep, well-drained soil. Avoid low areas or places surrounded by buildings or shade trees, where cold air settles. Also avoid planting where peach or cherry trees once grew.

  One mature, standard-size sour or sweet cherry tree will produce 30 to 50 quarts of cherries a year; a dwarf tree, about 10 to 15 quarts. Wait until the cherries turn fully red to harvest them; the sugar content rises dramatically in the last few days of ripening. Pick the fruit with stems attached, but be careful not to tear off the woody fruit spur, which will continue to produce fruit year after year.

Punica granatum

pomegranate

Deciduous, full sun, drought tolerant
- **CUISINE** The cultivation of pomegranates has been traced back to the ancient city of Samarkand, now in Uzbekistan. From there it was carried throughout Europe and Asia. The fruit is a symbol of fertility in many cultures and often forms part of special dishes and celebratory banquets in China, Greece, and the Middle East.
- **GROWING TIPS** Pomegranates form a neat, rounded shrub or small tree, and they bear showy orange-red flowers in spring after their brief, dormant, deciduous period. The new growth is also a pleasing bronze color, giving the plant even more cachet. There are also cultivars selected for their flower color with several variegated and double-flowered forms, and colors ranging from white to pinkish orange. There are even "dwarf" forms that produce miniature fruit that might not be a hit in the kitchen but are great for holiday decorations.
- **COOKING TIPS** Cooks around the world include pomegranate seeds in a variety of dishes, and its juice in beverages and sauces, or nibble on the crunchy seed. Great for jelly or an interesting salad dressing, pomegranate juice can also be used to make your own grenadine for flavoring and coloring drinks and sauces. Bring equal parts of juice and sugar to the boil.

Citrus fruit directory

Citrus trees are actually evergreen shrubs, retaining the majority of their leaves year-round. They are popular for their fantastically sweet, tart, and juicy fruits and also as a cooking ingredient with many uses.

In Mediterranean climates, citrus varieties are the most uniquitous evergreen fruits available to home gardeners. With their seductively sweet perfume and juicy fruits, they belong in any domestic orchard. Most citrus types are now available on several different rootstocks, so that some can be grown even in small spaces and in patio containers. For example, it's possible to grow a 'Washington' navel orange—grafted onto the appropriate rootstock—that is either 30 feet (9 m) tall, 15 feet (4.5 m) high, or just 5 feet (1.5 m). The tallest are known as "standard" trees and are about 20–30 feet (6–9 m) tall and wide, whereas "dwarf" trees will be about half that (or even less).

There are even smaller types that may reach only 7 feet (2.1 m) tall after a dozen years.

Citrus trees, being evergreen, are always sold in pots. Generally, buying the smaller size means that your tree can acclimatize to your native soil better and will generally catch up with the larger size in just a year or two. All require good drainage, so whether you plant them in your family orchard or grow them in a pot on your patio, dig in lots of well-rotted organic matter. These sturdy trees also require a high level of nitrogen. It's best to feed them through the growing season.

Citrus spp.

lime

Evergreen, full sun, regular water

- **CUISINE** Limes are almost as tart as lemons, but with a slightly different flavor.
- **VARIETIES** The juiciest and least cold-tolerant variety is 'Bearss', which is pale yellow when ripe. The famous 'Key Lime', also known as 'Mexican', has a distinctive, concentrated flavor. Kaffir lime has become very popular because of its use in Thai cooking. The Kaffir lime tree will reach 5 feet (1.5 m) tall, but because the leaves are constantly being picked for cooking, the plants usually remain small in size and are ideal for container growing.
- **GROWING TIPS** Lime trees should be planted on the south or southeast side of the house in order to take advantage of the cold protection provided by the house. For optimum growth and production, the trees should be planted in full sun. Keep trees well watered when the fruit is forming in spring and early summer. Ripe limes are usually still deep green, so pick only those that easily snap off the branch.

Citrus spp.

lemon

Evergreen, full sun, regular water

- **CUISINE** Most lemons have more acid than sugar and thus provide that tartness and citrus flavor to salad dressings, beverages, and baked foods. They also act as an efficient meat tenderizer.
- **VARIETIES** *Meyer* is sweet and extremely juicy. There is also a variegated selection, 'Pink Lemonade', with white-streaked leaves and pink flesh.
- **GROWING TIPS** Lemon trees need a sunny position away from all possible frosts. Growing near the house will help shelter your tree in colder weather. But, if the weather is going to drop below 30°F (1°C), you must wrap your lemon tree in a cozy blanket, or, preferably, bring it indoors. Growing lemon trees in containers works well, especially in a colder climate. Drag them into the conservatory or warm greenhouse during the winter months.

Citrus hystrix

kaffir lime

Evergreen tree, full sun, regular water
- **CUISINE** Unlike most citrus, both the leaves and fruits of the kaffir lime add zest to Thai and Cambodian dishes. Its flavor is distinct and can't be replicated by other ingredients. The bumpy skin of the fruit is used as a deodorizer, and the juice is reported to have anti-bacterial and insecticidal qualities.

Citrus paradisi

grape-fruit

Evergreen, full sun, regular water
- **CUISINE** The fruit takes at least 9 months to ripen, and may be even better after a year. The flesh may be pale to deep pink. Membranes are particularly bitter and need to be removed before eating.
- **VARIETIES** True grapefruit varieties need long, hot summers to develop their sweetest flavor. Hybrids such as the larger, inherently sweeter, pummelo are better for cooler zones.
- **GROWING TIPS** They grow best in a subtropical climate, where there are hot days and warm to hot nights during summer. The fruit ripens during fall and winter. If the trees are healthy and mature, they can withstand a few hours of temperatures below freezing point in winter, but after that time ice will form in the fruit, making it inedible.

Citrus reticulata

mandarin, tangerine

Evergreen, full sun, regular water
- **CUISINE** The sweet fruit is the easiest citrus to eat. It has loose skin that is very easy to peel, and the segments are easily separated to provide a bite-sized burst of citrus flavor.
- **VARIETIES** If planted alone, the seedless selections will have no seeds, or very few, but may produce seeds if planted near 'Valencia' oranges that can cross-pollinate with mandarins. Most mandarins naturally grow to only 12–15 feet (3.6–4.5 m) high, but varieties can be grafted on dwarfing rootstock for even smaller plants.
- **GROWING TIPS** Mandarins are very sensitive to frost, so it is best to grow a mandarin in early autumn or early spring. Thin out the branches in the center to allow sunlight and air circulation.

Citrus sinensis

orange

Evergreen, full sun, regular water
- **CUISINE** There are 2 major groups of sweet oranges. Those with a little indentation (actually an undeveloped twin fruit) are called "navel" oranges. 'Washington' is the best known variety. Navels are typically harvested in winter. The star of the citrus world is the second group, based on the 'Valencia'. It is widely planted and the best choice for juice. Fruits mature in late summer.
- **GROWING TIPS** Plant the tree in a warm, sunny area where the soil drains well. Mulch to conserve water. Water the tree deeply once every 7 to 10 days in midsummer. Water less often if it is rainy or cool. Harvest oranges when they taste sweet.

Fortunella sp.

kumquat

Evergreen, full sun, regular water
- **CUISINE** The kumquat has a thin, sweet peel and a zesty, tart center. The kumquat tastes best if it is gently rolled between the fingers before being eaten, as this releases the essential oils in the rind.
- **VARIETIES** Varieties include the nagami, the meiwa, and the marumi. The nagami is the the most tart but still edible straight from the tree, and the marumi has a soft, sweet rind.
- **GROWING TIPS** Needs regular fertilizer and moist soil for optimal growth.
- **COOKING TIPS** Kumquats don't need peeling to be eaten and apart from the pips are a perfect finger-sized citrus. Eat them as you would eat grapes.

Solanum quitoense

naranjilla

Small evergreen tree, full sun or partial shade, regular water
- **GROWING TIPS** This interesting fruit is from the deep tropics, but makes a good container plant indoors in more temperate zones. It will take many months to bloom and bear fruit wherever it is grown, but the fruits are a delicious blend of sweet and sour.
- **COOKING TIPS** Substitute the juice in any recipe where citrus is used.

Berries

Fruits of red and gold raspberries, and blackberries, are among the quintessential flavors of summer. Such luscious fruit makes it well worth braving the vicious thorns at harvesttime, though some thornless varieties are available.

Planting

Berry bushes are some of the easiest plants to grow, but they take maintenance to keep producing sweet, delicious berries. Follow these steps to ensure optimal fruit production and a successful season of gardening.

1 Plant the bare-root canes after the last frost in deeply prepared soil. Berries are one of the few plants that should be planted with their crowns below soil level. Cover them with 1 inch (2.5 cm) of soil and add a mulch after the new shoots appear.

2 All require a sturdy trellis to support their growth. Although canes grow to 6 feet (1.8 m) or more in length, the trellis needs only be 4–5 feet (1.2–1.5 m) high because the canes can be bent and tied in arching fans.

Pruning & tying

The necessary pruning and tying-in over late summer may produce a few scratches, but don't risk losing a good harvest in a couple of years by refusing to act. You might not even be able to walk down the rows between your canes if you let them get out of hand. Wear your toughest clothes, long sleeves, and gloves, and even protect your head if necessary, and cut all the canes that fruited in the current year to the ground in fall. Then tie up the new canes (those that grew the current spring and summer) that will bear fruit next year, and thin as necessary. For blackberries, leave only 12–16 of the sturdiest shoots from each original plant. Raspberries may be suckering farther away from the original crown, and you can thin them to 6–8 feet (1.8–2.4 m) apart. There may also be canes springing up in between the rows that need removing. Arrange the canes in a fan along the horizontal bars of the trellis after nipping off their tops at 6–8 feet (1.8–2.4 m) high. Use natural fiber ties, such as manila twine or sturdy cotton string, to make them easier to remove next year. Side shoots will grow from these main canes to produce next year's fruit, and need to be cut back to 1 foot (30 cm) in length in late winter or early spring before the flowering starts.

BLACK MAGIC

Blackberries aren't quite as enthusiastic growers as raspberries, but they will yield better with regular pruning. Blackberries can also have dangerous thorns. Gloves are recommended, and clean, sharp tools are also necessary. There are some modern blackberry varieties that are virtually thornless and they make pruning a lot less hazardous.

Growing strawberries

If you've ever eaten a strawberry fresh from the garden, you will know that there is a great difference between the store-bought and homegrown kinds in terms of flavor, juiciness, and color. Commercially grown strawberries also rely heavily on fungicides and other chemicals to keep their plants in shape. Although strawberries can be planted in spring, fall is also a great time to get them established. Planting then will result in more fruit instead of excess foliage next season. Many strawberries also like some winter chill, so a fall planting will give them a head start. Strawberries like evenly moist soil. If your garden is well drained, plant them in rows about 2 feet (60 cm) apart and space them 14–18 inches (35–45 cm) apart. If your soil stays soggy, then make raised mounds for planting them on. Plants may be available locally in the fall, but if not, buy them by mail order. The bare-root plants need to be kept damp on arrival and planted as soon as possible. Be sure to plant with the crowns exposed, because if they are covered with soil, they will rot. Mulch between the plants and rows to conserve moisture, reduce weeds, and keep the fruit, which develops just above the soil, clean.

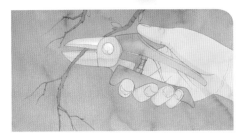

1 Use sharp pruning shears when pruning. If they are blunt, they crush and tear, leading to frost damage or disease.

2 Prune 3–4mm above buds so as not to damage them. Cut out any old or dead wood at the base of the plant to encourage strong new shoots from the base.

The plants spread by runners, and you can tackle them in various ways. If you want the parent plant to channel all its energy into producing large fruit, pinch off all the runners as they form. To increase the number of plants, allow some of the plantlets to grow and root. They should be spaced from 7 to 10 inches (18–25 cm) apart. After harvest, the older plants can be removed and the youngest allowed to stay for next year's crop. However, after three years or so, create a new bed with new plants to avoid any fungal diseases. Aphids, mites, slugs, and snails can also be a problem. The best solution for most of them is clean gardening practices and buying certified disease-free plants.

Strawberries can be grown in pots or raised beds with great success. There is even a special container called a "strawberry pot" with small pockets in the sides to receive the runners and root their plantlets, and it is ideal for kids of all ages.

Berries directory

Regardless of whether you have a large garden or no garden at all, it is possible for you to grow berries to enjoy fresh during the summer or frozen for the dark winter months.

Berries are some of the easiest fruits to grow in your home garden. They require very little attention, produce abundant masses of fruit each year, and the only pests you're likely to encounter are birds. Berries can be classified into two sub-categories: vine fruit and bush fruit. Cane fruit includes blackberries and raspberries. They are incredibly easy to grow, and if you prune them once a year, they'll grow masses of fruit for you for decades to come. Bush fruit include blueberries and gooseberries.

Organic feeds are best, as they don't impair the flavor of the berries or lower their nutritional value as chemical-based fertilizers do. They also help the plants grow at the rate they are supposed to, which leads to less risk of attack from pests such as aphids. Use a pelleted organic chicken manure or seaweed feed during the growing season, and mulch with an acidic dressing such as bark, sawdust, or leaf mold. Trap moisture in the ground in spring if you want to ensure soft and succulent summer fruits. Soft fruits are thin-skinned and will rapidly deteriorate if exposed to summer showers. Fall varieties of raspberry are the hardiest of berries—they can even withstand an early frost. Berry bushes don't require much maintenance, but be sure to prune back branches after the last harvest to encourage next year's growth.

Pick the fruit as it ripens, and cover with netting to protect from birds if necessary. Once you have started growing your own berries, you won't want to stop. They produce masses of fruit that you can eat raw, cook in desserts, or add to ice creams. And don't forget the health benefits of including berries in your everyday diet.

Fragaria
strawberry

Perennial, full sun to partial shade,
regular water

- **VARIETIES** Varieties of strawberries are either ever- or June-bearing. In cool, coastal regions, ever-bearing varieties will produce berries over the whole summer and may continue to bloom and set fruit as long as temperatures remain warm. In hot summer areas, with temperatures over 89°F (32°C), they will stop producing until it cools down again, in effect having a spring and a fall crop. The June-bearing varieties make one crop a year that peaks in early summer no matter where you grow them. Coastal gardeners may want to plant some of each to maximize their harvest.
- **GROWING TIPS** Mulch between plants after planting to keep the soil temperature cool, deter weeds, and keep the fruit off the soil. Straw is the traditional strawberry mulch. Do no use black plastic since it will raise the soil temperature and optimal fruit production requires cool soil.

Rubus idaeus and *R. occidentalis*
raspberry

Perennial vine, full sun, regular water

- **CUISINE** Unlike blackberries, tiny raspberry fruits do not remain connected to their core. When picked, they form a little hollow cup that is very fragile. When you see them on sale, they are usually nestled only two layers deep to preserve their soft shapes in small baskets or plastic containers. Growing them at home allows you to rush them from the garden to the table without fear of crushing the life out of them.
- **GROWING TIPS** Red and yellow raspberries were developed from *R. idaeus*, while black and purple types derived from *R. occidentalis*. Each type grows differently and requires slightly different treatment. The red and yellow types are called "ever-" or "fall-bearing." They produce two crops: one in the fall of the first year and another in the summer of the next year, after which the canes must be removed. The purple and black varieties grow much like blackberries, and when the 2-year-old canes have already borne fruit, they are removed.

Rubus spp.
blackberry

Perennial vine, full sun, regular water

- **CUISINE** Berries are clusters of individual seeds, each one surrounded by its own tiny fruit. As such, they contain a concentrated fruit flavor. Lightly sugared and scattered over ice cream, baked into a cobbler, or smoothed into jam and spread on toast, they are rich in flavor and color.
- **GROWING TIPS** Various species of blackberries have been domesticated in different parts of the world. Some are quite hardy and survive cold winter zones, so check that the rootstock is suitable for your location. The plants are perennial, but each cane, which grows from the central crown, is biennial and produces no fruit the first year, ceasing to produce any fruit after the second year. This growth pattern necessitates annual pruning to remove the old canes that have already borne fruit, and encourage the new ones.

Vaccinium spp.
blueberry

Perennial vine, full sun, regular water

- **CUISINE** Blueberries belong to the Azalea family and require similar growing conditions. The spine-less shrubs can be either evergreen or deciduous, vary from 3–10 feet (1–3m) in height, and are long lived (at least 30 years). The fruit has a waxy bloom, borne in clusters on the end of branches, and ripens from early summer to fall, depending on location and variety.
- **GROWING TIPS** An open, sunny, frost-free, sheltered position is best. Partial sun may do if full sun cannot be provided. Delay picking until the fruit is sweet. A blue berry is not necessarily a ripe berry, and ripening is uneven through the cluster.
- **COOKING TIPS** Blueberries can be used fresh, and store and freeze well. They can be dried, used for jellies and jams, pies, sauces, muffins, bread, pancakes, cakes, tarts, ice cream, juice, fruit salads, yogurt, and wine.

Ribes spp.
gooseberry

Perennial, full sun, regular water

- **CUISINE** Gooseberries are easy to grow and one of the earliest fruits of the year.
- **GROWING TIPS** Thin gooseberries in late May or early June, removing about half the crop. The fruits from this first harvest can be used for cooking. This will give a longer cropping season and leaves others more room to grow to a larger size. The second harvest can be done a few weeks later, and many of the fruits will be packed full of natural sugar and taste delicious. Never let plants go short of water when fruits are swelling and ripening. Heavy watering after a drought can cause fruits to split and rot. Wear gloves and long sleeves when harvesting the fruit to protect hands and arms from sharp thorns. Average yield from one gooseberry bush is between 8 and 10 pounds of fruit.
- **COOKING TIPS** Gooseberries used for culinary purposes such as tarts, etc., are usually picked underripe. A classic gooseberry concoction is a fool, made by folding cream into the stewed fruit. For dessert purposes, however, the fruit must be fully ripe.

Ribes nigrum
blackcurrants

Perennial shrub, full sun, regular water

- **CUISINE** Blackcurrants have traditionally been used for jams, pies, and puddings. More recently, there are varieties the size of small grapes that are tasty eaten by themselves, with ice cream or cream. Mixed with other fruit, they are also delicious.
- **VARIETIES** 'Ben Gairn' is one of the earliest varieties to fruit, and has medium-sized berries with a good taste. 'Ben Hope' grows taller than most blackcurrants, but it has the best flavor of all varieties.
- **GROWING TIPS** The best time to plant blackcurrant bushes is early winter, though they can be planted any time up to early spring as long as the soil is not water-logged or frozen. Do not prune the plants in the first winter after planting. In the second and subsequent winters, prune to encourage new growth. Blackcurrants are ready for harvest when the fruits are very nearly black. Always try to pick them in dry conditions—wet blackcurrants store very badly and will quickly turn moldy.

Climbing fruit directory

This selection of fruit covers all fruit growing as a climbing plant—kiwifruit, melon, grapes, figs, and passionfruit. They have the added attraction of making beautiful ornamental plants for your garden.

Vine fruits can be used to create a focal point and as a form of art. In an area where space is limited or where a plant is needed to accent a large blank wall, a climbing vine can be an outstanding landscape feature. A mature plant will catch the eye of almost any visitor to your home.

Climbing plants require support to mature properly and to allow for easy access for ongoing care and harvesting. There are many types of supports that you can use, ranging from small trellises to fancy arbors. One common and effective trellis method is to string wires between poles approximately 12 inches (30 cm) apart from each other. With this trellising system, all you have to do is periodically tuck the vines underneath the wires. Pull them up underneath to hold them up so the sunlight gets to the vines where the main part of the fruit is growing.

Actinidia deliciosa

kiwifruit

Perennial/deciduous, full sun, regular water

- **CUISINE** Kiwifruits are considered a "superfood" by many—they have more than twice the vitamin C of oranges, and as much potassium as bananas, and are good sources of magnesium, fiber, and vitamin E. They also have only 45 calories each. The large, deep green, leathery leaves are accompanied by cream-colored flowers that appear in midsummer. They turn orange-yellow as they age and are followed by 1½–2-inch (4–5-cm) fuzzy green fruits. The flesh, firm until fully ripe, is bright green or sometimes yellow, and the flavor is sweet/tart to acid, somewhat like that of the gooseberry.

- **GROWING TIPS** The plants need a long growing season (at least 240 frost-free days) that will not be hampered by late winter or early autumn freezes. Kiwifruit is an appropriate crop wherever citrus fruits, peaches, and almonds are successful. Kiwifruit plants need a substantial trellis, patio cover, or other permanent place to grow upon. Plant them in an area that is moist but well drained, and be sure that the soil does not become dry in hot weather.

Cucumis melo

melon

Annual and biennial, full sun, regular water

- **CUISINE** Melons are a summertime delight. They're versatile— more than a dessert or snack—as an ingredient in salads, salsas, side dishes, entrées, and drinks. Even the ripe seeds, dried and toasted, make a healthy snack.

- **VARIETIES** Plant what you, your neighbors and family will like, but use varieties that ripen over a period of the summer. Don't plant very much of any one thing on the same planting date, even if you like that variety, as they will all come on in a rush.

- **GROWING TIPS** In warm climates, sow melon seeds directly in the garden no earlier than 2 weeks before the last expected frost and when the soil temperature has reached about 70°F (12°C). Melons make good container plants if you choose a compact variety like 'Minnesota Midget' or 'Musketeer'. Use a container that's at least 2 feet (60 cm) deep, with good drainage. Fill it with good-quality potting soil enriched with compost, water plants frequently, and feed every 2 weeks.

Ficus carica L.
figs

Perennial, full sun, regular water

- **CUISINE** The fig is often thought of as fruit, but it is properly the flower of the fig tree. It is in fact a false fruit or multiple fruit, in which the flowers and seeds grow together to form a single mass.
- **VARIETIES** The best variety of fig tree to go for is 'Brown Turkey', whose fruit ripen in late August and have a reddish-brown skin, red flesh, and a sweet flavor. You can also try 'Brunswick', which ripens a few weeks earlier, and whose greeny-yellow skinned fruit have a sweet-tasting pink flesh.
- **GROWING TIPS** Prune the tree in late spring, removing shoots and buds that are pointing inward, as well as those pointing directly out from the wall, and any growths damaged by late frost. Remove debris and prunings, and apply a 4-inch (10-cm) deep layer of farmyard manure over the root area. Figs must be allowed to ripen fully on the tree before they are picked. They will not ripen if picked when immature. A ripe fruit will be slightly soft and starting to bend at the neck. Harvest the fruit gently to avoid bruising.

Passiflora edulis
passionfruit

Perennial, full sun or partial shade, regular water

- **CUISINE** The passionfruit vine is a strong, vigorous, evergreen climber, originating in South America. Passionfruit is generally eaten fresh but may be cooked for use in sauces and fillings. The pulp makes a delicious jam or jelly, and the seeds add a unique crunchy texture.
- **VARIETIES** There are 2 main varieties of passionfruit. The purple variety consists of huge red purple fruits with a silver speckle in the skin. The pulp is aromatic, sweet, and abundant. The yellow variety shares all of the characteristics of large size and long cropping with its purple sister. The only difference is the luscious golden color.
- **GROWING TIPS** Plant when the danger of frost is over. Soil that is waterlogged even for short periods increases the risk of root rot. Once established, passionfruit need regular feeding and deep watering to prosper. The fruit will quickly turn from green to deep purple (or yellow) when ripe and then fall to the ground within a few days. They can either be picked when they change color or gathered from the ground each day.

Vitis vinifera
grapes

Perennial/deciduous, full sun, regular water

- **CUISINE** The combination of crunchy texture and dry, sweet, tart flavor has made grapes an ever popular, between-meal snack as well as a refreshing addition to both fruit and vegetable salads.
- **VARIETIES** Grapes grow in clusters of 6 to 300, and can be crimson, black, dark blue, yellow, green, and pink. However, 'white' grapes are actually green in color, and are evolutionarily derived from the red grape. Grapes that are eaten as is or used in a recipe are called table grapes as opposed to wine grapes (used in viniculture) or raisin grapes (used to make dried fruit).
- **GROWING TIPS** Grapes need full sunlight and high temperatures to ripen, so plant on southern slopes, the south side of windbreaks, or the south sides of buildings. Avoid northern slopes and low ground since these will be cooler throughout the growing season, delaying ripening of the fruit.
- **COOKING TIPS** Grapes are commonly used to make jam, jelly, and wine. They are also used in foods marketed as being made without sugar, as they can add a wonderful natural sweetness. There are some points to remember about the flavor of different varieties when choosing which grapes to use in cooking: very large grapes tend to have a weak flavor; green grapes also tend to have a weak flavor; red grapes tend to have a fairly full flavor; purple grapes tend to have the flavor of red grapes plus a sort of harsher taste; and grapes with seeds tend to have better flavor than grapes without seeds.

Regional flavors

Each culture has its own distinctive methods of cooking and palate of flavors based on the indigenous foods and preferred spices. The key ingredient in any ethnic dish could be a certain spice, a fresh herb, or an unprepossessing root vegetable that lends texture to other, more universal ingredients such as eggs or pasta.

Travel in foreign countries brings many unique pleasures, especially new cuisines. Trying to replicate these recipes when you return home is not always easy. Certain ingredients may not be available, or they may be only in a packaged form with changes in taste, color, or texture. In more cosmopolitan cities, it may be easier to locate the special ingredients required to re-create ethnic dishes, but there's nothing like having your own source right outside your kitchen door. Luckily, many of these ingredients are undemanding to grow, and all lend an authentic flavor to ethnic dishes being created far from their place of origin.

Classic combinations from around the world draw on and combine the properties and distinct flavors of each herb.

South and Central America

The cuisine of Latin America stems from a mixture of different cultural backgrounds, regional foods, and cooking styles.

The focus of Latin American food is not on fancy sauces or the finest ingredients, but on feeding your family local ingredients and enjoying meals as a social occasion.

The love of cooking translates into a wonderfully flavorsome cuisine, and the staple ingredients include beans, tomatoes, tomatillos, cilantro, cumin, chilies, garlic, limes, rice, and potatoes, as well as herbs and spices such as epazote, heirba santa, verdolage, and naranjilla.

It is possible to grow all of these ingredients in your own home and bring a touch of the Latino spirit to your kitchen. A dish that blends Latin American ingredients and cooking styles is grilled chicken wraps with beans, tomatoes, and herbs.

Chicken and bean wraps

(Serves 4)

You will need:
- 4 skinless chicken breasts sliced into thin strips
- Chopped onion
- Chopped tomato
- 2 cloves of garlic, chopped
- 1 small bunch cilantro, minced
- Lime juice
- 2 tsp crushed cracked black pepper
- Stemmed jalapeno chilies
- ½ cup corn or olive oil
- 1 cup canned beans or black-eyed peas, rinsed
- ¼ cup sour cream
- 4 10-inch (25 cm) whole wheat tortillas
- 4 lettuce leaves

1 Place a large nonstick skillet over medium-high heat. Add oil and fry onions.
2 Add chicken and brown; add garlic and cook for a minute. Add beans and toss.
3 Remove from heat, drizzle some lime juice over, season with pepper, and sprinkle with cilantro.
4 Place lettuce leaf in the center of each tortilla and top with one-fourth of the chicken mixture. Sprinkle with some chopped tomato and chopped jalapeño chilies.
5 Top with sour cream and roll as you would a burrito. Slice in half diagonally and serve warm, with a wedge of lime. Garnish with cilantro.

North America

American cooking, quite simply, is the fusion of multiple ethnic or regional approaches into completely new cooking styles.

From the time the first settlers landed on the shores of the USA, immigrants to the country have brought their own recipes and traditions. Here they made do with, and adapted, the ingredients that were available, leading to a cuisine that, in many regions, has become quite unique. Hot dogs and hamburgers, for example, are both based on traditional German dishes, brought over to America by German immigrants to the States, but in their modern popular form they can be reasonably considered American dishes.

New York, with its diverse cultural mix, offers the most wide-ranging selection of cuisine from every part of the world. A profusion of delicatessens offers the most tempting dishes of peoples including Italians, Russians, and Greeks. New England cuisine is based upon the wonderful seafoods found in abundance on the coast, firm favorites being clam chowder, Boston baked beans, and lobster thermidor. Many dishes are typified by the use of dairy products and slow cooking methods.

The gold rush had one of the biggest influences on food in California and later the rest of the U.S. Chinese workers were brought in to work in the mines and railways, and it is here that the ubiquitous chop suey was born. Today Californian cuisine is a combination of many exotic influences from a wide variety of immigrant groups.

In the cuisine of the Midwest cattle ranching has been a major influence. Food is based on uncomplicated dishes such as pot roasts, sausages, ribs, and, of course, barbecue.

The Deep South is home to Cajun and Creole cooking, both associated with Louisiana in particular. Cajun cuisine features typical dishes such as jambalaya. Creole food offers delights such as gumbo, and red beans and rice. Other traditional southern foods include cooked greens, barbecued meats, and grits.

Finally, Tex-Mex, although found all over the States, originates in those states closest to the border with Mexico. Influenced heavily by immigrants from Africa, France, and Mexico, the dishes to be enjoyed in this style of cooking are enchiladas, burritos, and chili.

This recipe for authentic-tasting Southern-style fried chicken will show you how to make the best-tasting chicken you can imagine. Tender, juicy, and flavorful, all it needs for accompaniment is a bowl of crisp salad leaves from your garden.

Southern Fried Chicken

(Serves 4)

You will need:
- 8 chicken drumsticks
- 2 cubes chicken bouillon
- 3 cups (300 g) flour
- ½ onion, finely chopped
- 1 garlic clove, finely chopped
- ¼ tsp cayenne pepper
- 3 tbsp chopped fresh parsley
- 1 tbsp chopped fresh thyme
- 1 tsp salt
- 2 cups (500 mL) buttermilk
- vegetable oil
- salad leaves

1 Place the chicken legs in a saucepan. Cover with water, add the bouillon cubes, and bring to a simmer. Cook for 20–30 minutes, skimming off any foam and impurities that rise to the top during the cooking period. Remove the legs with a slotted spoon and set on a tray. Keep the liquid for use as a base for soup. Place the tray of chicken in the fridge and allow to cool down for half an hour.

2 Mix in a bowl the flour, onion, garlic, cayenne pepper, parsley, thyme, and salt. Put the buttermilk into another bowl. Dip each of the cooled chicken legs into the buttermilk. Then roll each one in the bowl of seasoned flour, to ensure that they are completely coated. Set aside.

3 Heat a generous amount of oil in a saucepan over medium-high heat. Add some of the chicken drumsticks to the hot oil and fry them for a couple of minutes, until the coating turns a lovely golden brown color. Remove and place on a tray lined with kitchen paper to drain. Add more oil if necessary and add another batch of chicken and fry. Cooking them in small amounts will ensure that the temperature of the oil remains constantly high. Continue to fry until all the legs are deliciously crispy! Serve the Southern Fried Chicken immediately with a crisp green salad made with homegrown salad leaves.

Africa

African cuisine is a mixture of native ingredients from a vast and varied landscape. The preparation is kept as simple as possible.

Africa is a huge continent consisting of everything from arid desert to subtropical wetlands, plains, and jungle. The great variety of African foods never ceases to amaze.

The eating habits of the different African regions vary greatly. Milk, curd, and whey make up the bulk of the diet in some areas, whereas in others milk cannot be produced because of cattle diseases. In East Africa, grains are a staple food, with meat rarely, if ever, being eaten, whereas in Central Africa beef and other meats are eaten with relish when available. Hunting for other food sources is also prevalent in forested areas. Meals with little meat are common across the continent, as are dishes with plenty of whole grains and beans, and even more fresh fruits and vegetables. Also look out for steamed greens, mixtures of hot spices with root vegetables, and the use of peanuts (used in everything from garnishes to soups). Melons, particularly watermelons, are also popular.

A traditional and delicious African dish, known as moi-moi, combines black-eyed peas, onion, tomato, peppers, sardines, and shrimp to make a sort of steamed cake that can be eaten either on its own or with rice.

Moi-moi

(Serves 2)

You will need:

- 2 cups black-eyed peas or 1 cup bean flour
- ½ onion
- 1 or 2 fresh peppers (chili or bell)
- 1–2 medium tomatoes (optional)
- 4 tsp vegetable oil
- Boiled egg
- 1–2 tbsp ground shrimp or prawns
- 1 can sardines in oil
- 1 tsp salt
- 2 –4 medium freezer bags or small aluminum cups

1. Put the black-eyed peas into a medium-sized pot and pour in enough water to cover. Soak overnight. In the morning, gently squeeze the peas as you wash them to remove the peelings. Place the cleaned peas in a blender and add half an onion, pepper, and 1–2 tomatoes, if desired. Blend until the mixture becomes a smooth paste or pudding.

2. If you are using already prepared bean flour, skip most of the above and just add your blended tomato, pepper, and onion to the flour and mix into a smooth paste.

3. Place the bean paste into a bowl and add 3–4 teaspoons of vegetable oil and stir. Chop the boiled egg and add it to this paste. Then add cooked shrimp or prawns, flaked sardines, and salt. Add about a cup of water to loosen the paste a bit.

4. Scoop the paste into freezer bags or aluminum cups, filling these not more than half their capacity to allow space for the bean mixture to expand once it is steamed. Tie the mouth of the bags and place in a cooking pot of water. Bring the water to a boil, then cover and simmer for about 30 minutes.

5. The cooked moi-moi looks like a baked cake. Allow to cool for about 10 minutes before serving. Serve with rice or eat as a main meal on its own.

Middle East and Mediterranean

The styles and flavors of Middle Eastern cuisine are quite distinct, despite encompassing many countries with different climates and cultures.

A typical Middle Eastern meal will start with the appetizers, known as meze—several tiny dishes with exotic morsels placed on the table all at once—which is a great way of appreciating the range of tastes on offer. There is an emphasis on big flavors, with succulent meat dishes being accompanied by salads, fresh vegetables, and always some kind of bread. Many spices and herbs (including cilantro, saffron, and chili) are used to give traditional recipes a kick-start.

The major difference between cooking techniques used in Middle Eastern and Mediterranean cookery is that in the Middle East meat is cooked slowly and for a long time, until it's very tender, except for kebabs, which are cooked quickly on skewers or on a grill.

Mediterranean cuisine, in contrast, is dominated by such vegetables as onions, eggplants, squashes, tomatoes, peppers, mushrooms, okra, and artichokes. Beans and lentils are also used extensively, and fresh herbs, including rosemary, basil, parsley, and oregano, add a distinctively Mediterranean fragrance and taste.

This dish cooks chicken pieces slowly in a flavorsome combination of artichokes, lemons, and olives for a real taste of the Middle East. Its name, tagine, derives from the earthenware pot used for cooking in Morocco; but any heavy-based pan can be used here.

Chicken Tagine

You will need:

- 3 tbsp olive oil
- 2 onions, chopped
- 2–3 cloves garlic
- ½ tsp saffron threads
- ½ tsp ground ginger
- I chicken, jointed
- Salt and pepper
- ½ lemon
- 2 tbsp cilantro, chopped
- 2 tbsp fresh parsley, chopped
- 2 small preserved lemons, peel only
- 12–16 olives
- 9 artichoke bottoms

You can buy frozen artichoke bottoms from Middle Eastern and Asian stores.

1 Heat oil in a wide casserole dish. Add onions and sauté over low heat, stirring, until softened. Stir in the garlic, saffron, and ginger. Add the chicken pieces in one layer, season, and pour in about 10 fl oz (300 mL) water. Simmer covered for about 20 minutes, occasionally turning the chicken and adding more water if necessary.

2 Lift out the chicken breasts and set aside. Continue to cook the remaining pieces for 25 minutes, then return the chicken breasts to the pan. Stir in the lemon juice, cilantro, parsley, preserved lemon peel, and olives. Then lift the chicken pieces and insert the artichoke bottoms in the sauce underneath. Add more water if necessary and cook for 10 minutes until the artichokes are tender.

Europe

A vast continent made up of many countries, Europe's tastes and flavors vary from place to place. Sauces are popular, and similar bases are adapted to suit the cooking styles of different regions.

Europe can be divided roughly into four main areas. First there is Eastern Europe, including Hungary, Poland, and the Russian Federation, with its hearty meat stews, frequent use of root vegetables, and fondness for smoky flavors. Northern Europe, including Great Britain and Scandinavia, favors rather more simple fare, and has a preference for meat and fresh produce. Southern Europe, including Greece, Portugal, Spain, and Italy, is famous for its sun-ripened ingredients and fantastic fish and seafood straight from the ocean. Finally, the cuisine of Western Europe, including France, Belgium, and Germany, places an emphasis on meat, but also specializes in delicious accompanying sauces and perfect patisserie.

Although these regions seem quite different from each other, they can be considered as one type of cuisine when compared with Asian cuisine. In Europe there is more emphasis on meat as the main part of the meal—in particular large joints of roasted meat.

One flavor associated with Southern Europe in particular is basil, an aromatic herb that flourishes in this region. To make the most of its delicious taste and pungency, try making pesto with homegrown basil as a sauce for pasta, grilled fish, or chicken, or use in a tomato sauce.

Tomato sauce

This is used all over Europe as a base for various dishes. In southern Italy oregano might be added. A Spanish variation uses fresh chilies.

(Serves 4)

You will need:
- 4 tbsp olive oil
- 2 large onions, chopped fine
- 3 garlic cloves, minced
- 8 diced tomatoes
- ¼ cup red wine
- ¼ cup chopped fresh herbs (herbs chosen will vary depending on choice or region and what is being served with the sauce)

1 Heat olive oil in a heavy skillet over medium heat. Add onion and garlic cloves; sauté until tender.

2 Add diced tomatoes with juices and wine and simmer for 10 minutes. Add chopped herbs and cook on a gentle heat for a further 5 minutes.

3 Remove from heat. Season sauce to taste with salt and pepper; cover to keep warm.

Turkish Cacık

A classic meze containing yogurt, dill, mint, cucumber, and garlic, this refreshing dish can be used as an appetizer or as a dip.

You will need:

- 2 cups plain yogurt
- 3 medium cucumbers, peeled and diced
- 2 cloves garlic, diced
- 1 tbsp dried mint
- a pinch of salt and pepper to taste
- 2 tbsp extra virgin olive oil

1 Place yogurt in a large bowl, add all other ingredients except salt and pepper, and mix thoroughly.
2 Add water until desired consistency is achieved.
3 Stir in some salt and pepper, taste, and add more if required. Serve at room temperature or chilled.

Scandinavian mustard-dill sauce

This is good with any fish and as a dressing for green beans. Boil the beans for 5 minutes, then rinse under cold water and dress with the sauce.

You will need:

- ½ cup Swedish or Dijon mustard
- 3 tbsp chopped fresh dill
- 1 tsp sugar
- 1 tbsp lemon juice or red wine vinegar, or to taste
- a pinch of salt and pepper to taste
- 2 tbsp vegetable oil

1 Whisk first 6 ingredients together in a bowl until smooth. Gradually add vegetable oil, whisking constantly, until blended and smooth.
2 Cover and let stand for 2 to 3 hours before serving to allow the flavors to develop.
3 Serve at room temperature or chilled.

Asia

The cuisine of this extensive region is packed full of fresh ingredients and differing regional cooking styles.

When you think of Asian cuisine and countries such as China, Thailand, Japan, and Korea, you are instantly transported to a world full of flavors, aromas, textures, and colors. The many herbs and ingredients used to create this melting pot of a cuisine are wide and varied, and combine to make the most wonderfully aromatic recipes.

The umbrella of the Asian region is far-reaching, and includes the freshness of sushi in Japan, the heat of a coconut curry in Thailand, the hearty stews of Mongolia, the spiciness of a Sri Lankan stir-fry, and the noodle dishes of Malaysian cooking. A multitude of ingredients is used, with chilies, lemongrass, and ginger heading a long list. The cooking often focuses on speed and fresh ingredients, as in stir-frying, which ensures that the maximum flavor is retained.

A particularly fragrant and mild prawn curry originating in Goa provides a perfect example of the fusion of flavors and ingredients that we associate with Asian cuisine. It is also an ideal way of using homegrown coriander.

Jhinga Caldeen (Goan Prawn Curry)

Any form of fresh, firm fish such as monkfish or shark may be used instead of prawns.

You will need:
- 1 cup (400 g) fresh, cooked peeled prawns
- ½ tsp salt
- 2 tbsp white wine or cider vinegar
- 1 tsp cumin
- 2 tsp dried coriander
- 1 tsp turmeric
- ¼–½ tsp chili powder
- ½ tsp black pepper
- 3 tbsp sunflower oil
- 1 onion, finely chopped
- 1-in (2.5-cm) cube ginger root, chopped
- 4–6 cloves garlic, peeled and crushed
- 8 fl oz (250 mL) warm water
- 2–4 green chilies, sliced and deseeded
- ½ tsp salt
- 1 cup (90 g) coconut milk
- 2 tbsp chopped cilantro

1 Put the prawns in a bowl, add the salt and vinegar, and leave for 10–15 minutes. Mix the spices together in a small bowl and set aside. Gently fry the onion in the oil until pale golden, stirring constantly. Add ginger and garlic and fry for another minute. Add mixed spices and fry for another minute.

2 Add the water, chilies, salt, and coconut, cut into pieces. Simmer until the coconut dissolves. Add prawns and cook for 2–5 minutes, depending on the size of prawn. Add half the chopped coriander leaves and remove from heat. Garnish with rest of the coriander. Serve with plain boiled rice.

Pacific Rim

Influenced by the cuisine of several continents, the food of the islands of the Pacific Rim is a rich fusion of many cuisines brought from all over the world.

New Zealand cuisine is derived from various sources, especially British and Maori, the United States post–World War II, and Australia, Southeast Asia, and India. New Zealand cuisine emphasizes the quality and freshness of ingredients produced on land and in the sea, which is readily available in an island nation that bases its economy on agriculture. Similar to the cuisine of Australia, the cuisine of New Zealand is traditionally "meat and three veg" and increasingly modified by Mediterranean and Pacific Rim tastes as the country becomes more cosmopolitan, albeit at a more gradual pace than Australia. Modern cuisine of Hawaii is a fusion of many cuisines brought by multi-ethnic immigrants to the islands, particularly of Chinese, Filipino, Japanese, Korean, Polynesian, and Portuguese origins, and including food sources from plants and animals imported for Hawaiian agricultural use from all over the world.

Tropical chicken salad

(Serves 8)

You will need:
- 4 pineapples halved lengthwise
- 2 cups fresh pineapple, diced
- 4 cups cooked and drained black-eyed peas (or canned)
- 2 mangos, peeled and diced into ½-inch squares
- ½ cup chopped red bell pepper
- ¼ cup chopped spring onions
- 6 cups cooked tiny shell macaroni
- 2 jalapeño peppers, seeded and chopped
- ½ cup chopped cilantro
- 4 boneless, skinless chicken breasts marinated in tequila, lime juice, salt, pepper, cumin, and cayenne pepper, barbecued until golden

For the dressing:
- 1 tbsp roasted garlic oil
- 1 cup peanut oil
- 2 tbsp honey
- 1 tsp ground cumin
- 1 tbsp rice wine vinegar
- 1 tbsp sweet chili paste
- juice of 2 limes
- 1 tbsp triple sec
- 2 tsp sea salt
- 2 tsp white pepper
- 1 tsp green jalapeno tabasco sauce

1 Place dressing ingredients in a jar and shake well.
2 Pour over salad, toss, and chill for 2 hours.
3 Fill pineapple shells with the salad. Slice the chicken breasts crosswise, and serve on top of the salad.

Suppliers

UK

www.organic-gardening.net
www.organiccatalog.com/catalog/
www.gardenorganic.org.uk
www.organicmatters.co.uk
www.haxnicks.co.uk
www.seedfest.co.uk

US

www.amishlandseeds.com
www.gardeners.com
www.hydroasis.com
\www.outdoorlivingsupplies.com
www.tmseeds.com
www.johnnyseeds.com
www.thegardener.com

AUSTRALIA

www.organicdownunder.com
www.soilsaintsoils.com.au
www.greenharvest.com.au

www.gardengrove.com.au
www.peatssoil.com.au
www.gardenersdirect.com.au

INFORMATION SITES

www.poppymercer.com
www.organicgardeningguru.com
www.organicgardeninfo.com
www.motherearthnews.com
www.hgtv.com
www.helpfulgardener.com
www.gardening.about.com
www.gardenersworld.com
www.garden.org
www.bbc.co.uk/gardening/basics/techniques/organic_index
www.backyardgardener.com
www.abc.net.au/gardening/features/organic_gardener.htm
www.organicgardening.com

Acknowledgments

The genesis of this book began long ago with my enjoyment of gardens, especially those that produce delicious edibles. For that I must thank my family, in particular my grandfather, who fed our families for years with fresh and healthy food from his garden. By eating such superior fruits and vegetables, I learned to plant and harvest my own gardens. I also want to thank the many people who have encouraged me to write about plants and gardens. There are too many to list here, but their comments and questions have provided continuing support for my work.